Please return or renew by
latest date below

The Canadian Condominium

Domestic Issues and External Policy

Thomas A. Hockin *et al.*

MCCLELLAND AND STEWART LIMITED

0-7710-4181-0

The Canadian Publishers
McClelland and Stewart Limited
25 Hollinger Road, Toronto 374

Printed and bound in Canada

Contents

1974/(E-0427)/X-7

Acknowledgements

This page constitutes an extension of the copyright page. For permission to reprint copyright material, grateful acknowledgement is made to the following copyright holders and publishers.

Canadian Business Magazine, Montreal, for Paul St. Pierre, "Industry Too Timid in ECC Market," *Canadian Business Magazine*, February, 1971

Canadian Institute of International Affairs, Toronto, for Douglas M. Johnston, "Canada's Arctic Marine Environment: Problems of Legal Protection," from *Behind the Headlines*, XXIX (5-6), July, 1970; and for Lorne Kavic, "Canada and the Pacific," from *Behind the Headlines*, XXIX, May, 1970, reprinted with permission from Lorne Kavic

Canadian Journal of Economics, Toronto, for Table 2, from R. Marvin McInnes, "The Trend of Regional Income Differentials in Canada," *Canadian Journal of Economics*, May, 1968

The Institute of Public Administration of Canada, Toronto, for Table 1, reprinted from, D. V. Smiley, "The Structural Problem of Canadian Federalism," *Canadian Public Administration*, Vol. 14, No. 3, Fall, 1971. Reprinted by permission of the Institute and Professor Smiley

The Chairman's Preface

This document emerges from the June 12, 13, 1971 panel meeting of Canadians and non-Canadians who met to discuss Canadian external relations and domestic developments for the 1970's. The study was sponsored by Georgetown University's Center for Strategic and International Studies, which is supported by private, not government, funds. The study was conducted to improve the general understanding of Canada in the United States and to expose Canadians to some perceptions of Canada held by non-Canadians. This study did not attempt to produce specific policy recommendations or to divine specific government intentions, its aim was simply to provide general background so that the average American can better understand Canada's external posture and domestic developments.

Because of the nature and amount of information and comment which the meeting engendered, the decision was made to publish this material in its entirety for the benefit of a wider Canadian public.

A special word of thanks is due to Professor Thomas A. Hockin, the research director and principal author of this volume. The work of the panel and this entire project owe a very great deal to the scholarship and industry of Professor Hockin.

John J. Deutsch
Panel Chairman

Introduction

The following material is a modest attempt to introduce some of the salient issues which may affect Canadian external policy, directly or indirectly, in the 1970's. Except for some updating made in order to reflect events since June 12 and 13, 1971, the content is similar to that prepared as background reading for the panelists who met in Quebec City to discuss Canada's domestic and external policy.

Except for two or three members, the panelists were not experts on Canadian foreign policy. Rather, they were chosen because they were thoughtful representatives of certain outlooks and regions in Canada, and could respond to the issues of Canadian external policy from a particular perspective. There were also representatives on the panel from the United States, Britain, South America, and Japan, and they reacted to the Canadian dilemmas and opportunities from the perspective of their national or international experience.

Hence the introductory nature of some chapters. They were addressed to those who might well be considerably well informed on some of the issues or topics raised, but who would welcome introductory background on the other issues as well. The reader of this volume should not search for bold new interpretations or path-breaking sets of research findings. Its purpose is simply to introduce some of the key issues relating to Canadian external policy.

It can be claimed, however, that much of the background material, the *Findings*, and the panelists' comments do discuss Canadian external policy in a way somewhat different from the usual discussions conducted by those primarily interested in this field. Special attention is given to Canada's domestic characteristics because here will be found some of the more important imperatives affecting Canada's external priorities, especially since the first priority of Trudeau foreign policy is to "increase Canada's economic growth," and the second is to enhance Canadian independence. This leads to an undisguised emphasis in the discussion of Canada's economic development, that to de-industrialize Canada's economy and to depend on resource extraction is an increasingly untenable position for Canada in the 1970's. To be so concerned, may appear to some Canadian observers to show little more than a reassuring grasp of the commonplace. Yet such an understanding seems little in evidence in the attitude towards Canada in many foreign capitals, and thus it deserves special mention here. These domestic characteristics (economic and otherwise), are organized under four topics for consideration: the nature of the asymmetry and cohesion in the Canadian federal arrangement; the momentum of the provinces' quest for economic growth; the political, social, and economic stresses in Quebec; and the problems involved in an industrial strategy for Canada as a whole. This is followed by a discussion of specific external issues including trade, Canadian-American relations, and the changing nature of Canada's foreign policy in general.

As the research director for this volume, I wish to thank Ken McRoberts who authored Chapter 3, and Gerald Wright who was co-author with me on Chapter 7. I wish to thank Christine DeWolfe and David Crane for their research help on two other chapters; and also Sandra Mark for her typing skill. Special thanks are due to Dr. John Deutsch and Jon Vondracek for their help and encouragement throughout. Special gratitude should be extended to the Georgetown University Center of Strategic and International Studies which sponsored the study and gave me, as research director, complete freedom to put whatever I wished into this book, as well as extending the same freedom to Dr. Deutsch in his choice of panelists.

Thomas A. Hockin

Chapter 1

Federal Asymmetry and National Cohesion in the 1970's

It is well known that domestic sources of foreign policy are no less crucial to its content and conduct than are the international situations toward which it is directed. This reality is unavoidable for anyone concerned about Canadian foreign policy in the 1970's. It is vital therefore to comprehend the way in which Canada sees itself, and solves its problems, in order to understand how domestic imperatives might affect foreign policy. This, and the following two chapters will introduce some of the more important imperatives and restraints. This chapter is intended primarily as an introduction for the non-Canadian reader since most of what follows is well known to most Canadians. Although there may be an awareness outside Canada of the "Quebec" problem, some of Canada's other problems of regional fragmentation are less well known. Also, there may be little under-standing of the cohesive elements because of the heavy emphasis on fragmentation. What follows, then, is an introduction to some elements of political fragmentation and cohesion as Canadians see them.

Much of the essence of political and social Canada is *Habitat*, the residential condominium erected amidst the glitter of Canada's Expo '67. *Habitat* has had an impact on the international architectural imag-ination far more than most Canadians realize. Perhaps part of the rea-son for its impact is that it expresses the contemporary values and or-ganization of Canada (and to some extent other nations) to an extraor-dinary degree. For indeed, better than any concept of an inert mosaic, today's Canada manifests the structural and social attributes of a con-temporary condominium.

Like the modern condominium concept, Canada is by definition a multiple unit organization comprising individual components that afford a high degree of social, economic, and political diversity. The binding forces are both material and societal, for Canada is a massive geography sparsely settled, tied together by the hardward of technology, and politically allied through a system of federal-provincial prerogatives. As presently constituted, the system seems to allow for considerable social, economic, and political value asymmetry among the provincial components, and it seems to serve to resist the temptation of social homogenization on the one extreme and political balkanization on the other.

Moreover, the life of Canada, like the life of a condominium, is not a medium for total retreat into a private utopia. Each unit needs some co-operation and intercourse with the other and the organization itself is not designed to be totally self-sufficient within its surrounding community. The economic, social, political, and constitutional ties of the provinces to the federal government are considerable, and now Canada's external relations are also vital to their livelihood.

In trying to comprehend Canada as a whole, it may be instructive first to examine the differences within the country that make the constituent parts distinctive and asymmetrical, and which to some extent move us from a condominium reality to something far more complicated yet not entirely different from that reality.

The provinces vary in size and population; each province exhibits dissimilar economic features (indicated in Chapter 2); the meaning of "federal-provincial relations" varies for each province and apart from the obvious differences between Quebec and the other provinces, there are other significant variations in social groupings and cultural patterns. Let us introduce the differences in federal-provincial relations first.

British Columbia has traditionally felt somewhat isolated geographically and economically from eastern Canada, and thus far has had less to gain from Canada's present tariff structure than most other provinces. Federal jurisdiction has, in part, affected the province's relations with the United States, as well as its economy, based as it is on resource and coastal industries.

The Prairies depend on Ottawa for vigorous export programs on behalf of grain and other products. Alberta's wealth, but unusual dependence on the oil and gas industries, and its small manufacturing sector give it priorities somewhat different from Saskatchewan and

Manitoba, which are less wealthy and continue to show a frequent need for federal assistance on welfare and regional incentive programs. In short, the relationship of each western province to the federal government differs somewhat, but the need for some relationship, even for promoting provincial priorities, is obvious. The birth and continuance of various protest political parties—populist, agrarian, socialist and Social Credit—in the West, is a function, in part, of central Canada's neglect and ignorance of the particular needs of the West where, for example, freight rates, lower tariffs, and tax policy on resources, are key issues. Wealthy Ontario, with its industrial diversity, ranks such issues low on its lists of priorities.

The dependence of the maritime provinces on the federal government, however, is even more obvious. As the 1971 Deutsch report on Maritime Union shows, the dependence of the maritime provinces on federal subsidies, grants and incentives for economic expansion and other purposes turns them, in some instances, almost into wards of the federal government. Quebec's concern for its culture has always made it jealous of federal invasions into what it deems to be provincial jurisdiction. And the expanding notion of the meaning of "culture" in Quebec has led, increasingly since 1960, to major tests of the meaning of Canadian "federalism."

These differences in the federal-provincial relationship from province to province contribute to the asymmetry of Canada's political structure in the sense that "federal-provincial relations" can mean very different things, depending on the province you are examining. Donald Smiley (in *Canadian Public Administration*, Fall 1971, pp. 329-330), has summarized the major conflicts in Canadian politics along territorial lines as follows:

1. *Those related to interprovincial and interregional equalization by the federal government.* In recent years equalization has been extended much beyond the Rowell-Sirois recommendation [in 1941] that each province should have at its disposal adequate revenues to provide services at national average levels without imposing on its citizens taxation at rates above the national average. Equalization now involves a complex of federal and federal-provincial programs to encourage economic growth and enhance economic opportunities in the less favoured parts of Canada, particularly in Quebec and the Atlantic provinces.

2. *Those related to national economic policies.* The traditional

economic cleavages between central Canada and the peripheral provinces to the east and west of the heartland remain, even though the peripheral economies–and in particular those of western Canada –have become more diversified. These continuing conflicts involve national trade, transportation and monetary policies as well as newer differences with respect to the development and sale of natural resources.

3. *Those relating to cultural duality in Canada.* The response of the provinces with English-speaking majorities to the French fact in Canada is most positive in those with large French-speaking minorities and least so where this minority is small. These differences are evident whether the claims of duality are expressed through recognition of the two official languages, some sort of special arrangement for Quebec or support for constitutional revision.

If we classify the interests and policies of the provinces toward each of these areas of conflict the result is something like that shown in Table 1. In these terms, Quebec and the western provinces are

Table 1.   Areas of Conflict

	Contending Provinces		Provinces whose attitudes are ambiguous
Interprovincial equalization	Quebec and the Atlantic provinces	Ontario Alberta BC	Saskatchewan Manitoba
National economic policies	Quebec Ontario	Atlantic and western provinces	
Cultural duality	Quebec Ontario New Brunswick	BC Alberta Saskatchewan Newfoundland	NS Manitoba PEI

Source: Table and quotation printed by permission of the Canadian Institute of Public Administration, and Professor Smiley.

ranged against each other on each of the axes of conflict. This conflict is more marked in the case of Alberta and British Columbia
than in Saskatchewan or Manitoba. These two latter provinces are
on the borderline between "have" and "have not" provinces and if
favourable economic circumstances should push them toward the
former category the country would be clearly divided on the issue of
interprovincial equalization by the Ottawa River.

Also contributing to asymmetry in federal-provincial relations and
in the character of each province is the persistence of local identities.
Such loyalties are, of course, unmistakable in Quebec, but they seem
to remain strong in all parts of Canada except Ontario. For example,
in a nation-wide survey of Canadian attitudes (carried out at the end
of 1969 by a daily newspaper), the following patterns were exposed:

In the maritimes no less than 52 per cent of the people thought of
themselves first as Nova Scotians or New Brunswickers or Prince
Edward Islanders, and only afterwards as Canadians. 34 per cent
of the people in the prairie provinces declared their local loyalties
stronger than their national ones; 28 per cent of British Columbi-
ans felt their land within the mountains more important than Canada; only in Ontario, which identifies with the concept of Confederation more closely than any other region was the fraction of local
patriots negligible.[1]

Other factors contribute to various depths of regional cleavage in
political, social, and economic attitudes in Canada. Since the turn of
the century the four western provinces have been distinguished from
Canada's other provinces in their high proportion of foreign-born
inhabitants. (Although the foreign-born population of Ontario has
been growing since World War II as well.) The tendency of each
province to develop around the key metropolitan centre (with few
counter-pulls to cities outside the province) may yield considerable
political allegiance to provinces as political units. This experience,
according to Canadian historian J. M. S. Careless, contributes to
"limited identities" in Canada and therefore is somewhat in contrast
to the American experience of homogenization of political attitudes
through urbanization.

Also, the conflict between interests of primary versus secondary
industry in Canada tends to be reflected by provincial boundaries.

[1] Quoted by George Woodcock in *Encounter* (Spring, 1971), p. 82.

Conflicts will arise, for example, between provinces oriented to primary industry such as British Columbia and Alberta, with Ontario, which is geared to secondary industry. A further source of conflict is that the other regional economic cleavage, the *per capita* income differential, has diminished very little, if at all, over the past forty years. This suggests that "a high level of national economic growth," the highest priority of economic policy of federal governments since World War II, has not reduced regional disparities and therefore entrenches regional antagonisms to central Canada.[2]

Table 2. Relative Levels of *Per Capita* Income Canada and Regions, 1926-1962

Canada = 100

Years	Maritimes	Quebec	Ontario	Prairies	British Columbia
1926-27	64	86	115	107	120
1930-32	70	95	126	73	126
1940-42	68	88	124	86	122
1950-52	64	82	118	106	118
1960-62	65	86	118	96	114

Source: R. Marvin McInnis, "The Trend of Regional Income Differentials in Canada," *Canadian Journal of Economics*, (May, 1968), p. 445. Reprinted by permission.

Yet even with these local loyalties, Canada, like other asymmetrical federal societies, holds together. The severest test to unity is Quebec and this will be discussed subsequently. Here, however, it is vital to recognize some of the elements that contribute to cohesion in Canada because they perhaps explain how the condominium stays together in spite of the economic cleavages and limited identities in Canada.

General theories of national and regional integration, such as those of Karl Deutsch, Ernst Haas, and others, emphasize the role of economic linkages, fears of external enemies, cultural affinities, common historial consciousness, and increased communication as the primary determinants behind integration. All of these factors are important when examining political cohesion in Canada and can be used, in

[2] See R. Alford, *Party And Society* (Chicago: 1963), Chapter 9, for data from 1945 to 1962. For data on poverty see the *Senate Report on Poverty* (Ottawa: 1971), and the *Last Post's*, "Renegade Report on Poverty" (July, 1971).

a formal theory of the Canadian condominium, to explain the amount of Canadian cohesion that presently exists. Other elements are also important and because they tend to get overlooked or hidden in formal theories of integration or cohesion they will be suggested here.

As the French say of Alsace-Lorraine, "think of it always, but speak of it never." Canadian federal political leaders are constantly aware of the possibility of Quebec separating but do not encourage self-fulfilling prophesy by discussing the possibility very much. All federal Canadian political parties advocate what they call "national unity." The term has many meanings, but the common denominator of them all is the notion of "holding Canada together" not by force, but by consent. All federal parties and all major provincial parties, except one in Quebec, appear to support this notion.

Canadians have a degree of ideological unity in the sense that the Canadian acceptance of the sphere of government is extensive in all regions of Canada. Fear of government in Canada appears far less pronounced than in the United States. This may explain in part why Canada appears to have less class voting than the U.S., Britain, or Australia, for example. The three major political parties have accepted the fact that governments must give leadership for national and provincial development and for more equitable distribution. (With yet 4.5 million Canadians classified as living in poverty in 1971, it is possible that conditions for more class consciousness may be developing and will push for government action that may be far more fundamentally redistributive than in the past.)

At the level of public advocacy and public philosophy, there seems to be an agreement that Canada should strive not to be a cultural melting pot but something like a condominium. This may help to lessen slightly feelings of local and cultural xenophobia, although there are at least three sets of qualifications to any pure condominium reality. First, a large part of French-Canada doubts whether this public disclaimer of homogenization by English-speaking Canada is candid, or if candid, meaningful. Second, the public philosophy of the mosaic or condominium can be a cover for keeping ethnic groups separate and therefore for keeping certain ethnic groups out of positions of national or provincial influence presently dominated by Anglo-Saxon or French-speaking Canadians. This, in a sense, was what former Canadian Prime Minister John Diefenbaker opposed; what he called "hyphenated-Canadianism." Third, it would be an unusually generous description of Canadians as a people to assume that their public commitment to a condominium for the sake of the nation as a whole implies a personal commitment of cultural tolerance by individual Canadians within their own "living unit," their own social life, or even in their own city, town, or village. The problems faced by Canadian Indians, Orientals, and Blacks in Canada raise questions about such a commitment.[3]

At the level of past and present public rhetoric, and political, as well as historical imagination, it seems clear that there is a notion of Canada as a northern nation. Canadian national feelings, like the national impulses in other countries, have been expressed, to quote one historian "in myths and legends about the past and anticipation of noble missions in the future," as well as in distinctive economic and international policies.[4] The idea of Canada as a northern nation is part of this. The drive for sovereignty in the Arctic, for development of the North, is no ephemeral Canadian topic; it is probably part of the country's definition of itself. It also supplies, for some, a frontier-like romance that has its base in a communitarian as well as in an individualist spirit.

A majority of Canadians share a disinclination to join the United States. This disinclination varies in intensity and degree from region to region in Canada, but a clear majority of all provinces express this feeling, especially since the increase in American foreign and domestic problems. This proclivity to avoid joining one's neighbour in political form should not be under-estimated by students of regional integration anywhere, but should be particularly noted in the case of Canada. For example, Swiss unity has been explained in part by the Swiss-Italian disinclination to join Italy, the Swiss-German disinclination to join Germany, and the Swiss-French disinclination to join France. Canada's disinclination was perhaps at its weakest in the first and fifth decades of this century, but with the rise of nationalist groups in the 1970's it appears obvious that even "continentalism without political integration" is losing popularity. (See the Canadian Gallup polls in the *Toronto Star*, February 12, and February 16, 1972, showing that 67 per cent of Canadians believe there is enough U.S. investment in Canada, and that 69 per cent favour a screening agency for new foreign investment).

[3] See, for example, Robin Wink's, *The Blacks in Canada* (Montreal: 1971); and also a sensitive Hon. B. A. thesis of Winston Chao, "The Chinese Community in Toronto" (York University: 1971).

[4] See Carl Berger's Chapter in P. Russel, ed., *Nationalism in Canada* (Toronto: 1964). For the community argument see, for example, Jim Lotz, "The Myth of the Rich North," *Canadian Forum* (January, 1969).

Canadian political scientists are beginning to recognize that élite accommodation at all levels (labour, business, agriculture, cultural, etc.) may make it possible for political leaders to hold the country together and to maintain and operate the political system by co-operating among themselves.[5] Today there are some serious doubts about the extent to which Quebec's élites are taking part in this process of accommodation, but many of them are doing so and this helps to contribute to Canadian cohesion. The various élites at the federal level are drawn from regional sub-cultures, whose leaders seem to agree on the desirability of maintaining the system while the mass of people in the regional sub-cultures trust and support these élites. Some Canadians have argued that élite accommodation holds Canada together far better than would any attempt to arrive at a homogenized set of mass-supported political standards. Yet there is a growing awareness in Canada of class arguments, and since a class argument helps to put unorganized groups back into the picture, it tends to de-emphasize formal élites. This awareness may even establish some mass-supported economic-political standards and make some types of élite accommodation and balancing less necessary.[6]

Another important reality about cohesion in Canada in the 1970's is that the notion of Canadian "independence" may be deepening. Early notions of Canadian independence usually emphasized what appear in the 1970's to be far less potent activities: the notion of independence in the British Empire then Commonwealth; then the idea of independence through the attributes of a diplomatic presence (the opening of missions abroad in the 1940's, appointing a separate Secretary of State for External Affairs and a world trip by a Canadian Prime Minister, etc.). Independence in the 1950's and early 1960's began to mean "distinctiveness of behaviour," that is, the divergence of Ottawa's policies from Washington was often taken as a "measure of independence." Now, however, a large section of the Canadian community is actively engaged in attempts to achieve more Canadian economic, social and political independence from the United States. For example, most Canadian universities are now attempting to increase their Canadian faculty representation and the Canadian content of their curriculum. The Canada Council, the National Film Board, the National Film Corporation, and countless other federal

---

[5] Several Canadian political scientists, notably Sid Noel, are developing this approach to understanding Canadian political cohesion. See the symposium published in the *Canadian Journal of Political Science* (March, 1971).

[6] See the arguments in Charles Taylor, *Pattern of Politics* (Toronto: 1970).

organizations are attempting to improve opportunities for Canadian experience to express itself. Already there has been aid to Canadian book-publishing and restrictions on foreign magazine and book distribution in Ontario and perhaps most notable are the recent actions by the CRTC (Canadian Radio and Television Commission) to ensure that a proportion of ordinary and prime time broadcasting on Canadian television and radio networks is of Canadian origin.

Another increment that the Trudeau Government hopes may lead to some cohesion is the new tendency of federal Cabinet committees and the Public Service to *plan* policy on the basis of "broad national problem areas" and to concentrate on the "supra-regional" necessities for policy instead of postponing planning because of partial or concurrent provincial jurisdiction over such areas as welfare, environment, municipal affairs, etc. The Trudeau Government has intensified this trend to supra-regional planning through program budgeting, through Cabinet reorganization by function and issue-area, and by the perspective of the planning and priorities network of the Privy Council Office and the Treasury Board. This approach may or may not work. Quebec's former deputy minister of Inter-governmental Affairs, Claude Morin, shrewdly describes how this process works. When asked if the Trudeau Government was "centralist" he replied in an interview in the *Financial Post* (August 14, 1971, p. 5):

> The forces are much more subtle now. Ottawa doesn't attack frontally, but from the side. They won't create a municipal affairs department but they do set up a secretariat of urban affairs. Then a couple of years later it becomes a department – same thing in the environment field. They invade areas by osmosis, through their financial and structural powers. It's not the same type of centralism. It puts the emphasis on the problem areas of the future. But the results are the same.

One of the most fundamental yet widespread errors of American (and of some Canadian) judgements on Canada's viability as a nation is the tendency to equate the amount of conflict and fragmentation in Canada's political society with the extent of Canadian willingness to be politically, culturally, and economically absorbed by the United States. This erroneous equation is often left unquestioned by both the political élite and by its most radical critics in Canada.

The equation is misleading and can lead to profoundly inaccurate perceptions of North American reality. The forces suggested above which contribute to political cohesion and to fragmentation in Canada are merely the tip of the iceberg. These forces are supplemented by a number of other vitalizing ideas and forces – cultural, economic, psychological, and historical – which if difficult to describe are nonetheless real. It would do violence to their subtlety to attempt to summarize them here. Yet they spring from the uniqueness of Canadian geography and history, and from Canadian social and political organization and ideas, as much as from the so-called common "North-Americanness" of Canadians and Americans. Canadian visual arts, poetry, literature, and historiography show this uniqueness in the realm of ideas, for example. There are themes of experience and of imagination in Canada, which if they do not add up to a Canadian political consensus, adds up to a nation which is completely misunderstood if viewed merely as a North American extension of American ideas and experience. These give a sense of place and meaning to many Canadians.[7]

If Canada became a "statist" society with all social and political values defined and enforced by political leaders, there is no doubt that some definition of Canadian uniqueness would be proclaimed to Americans and to others. Yet this definition would of course be little more than an intolerable vulgarization and would, in the long run, command little credibility. Foreign countries, especially the United States, should not have to be jolted by such vulgarizations in order to recognize a nation's will to survive and its uniquely-felt characteristics. If, for example, Canada and the United States are to enjoy mutual understanding and respect it is not perhaps too one-sided to suggest that the United States must try better to understand these characteristics of uniqueness and persistence and the emerging imperatives of nation-building which face Canada this decade.

NATIONAL COHESION AND FOREIGN POLICY

The relevance to external policy of any of these elements of cohesion is not easy to trace with assurance. One conclusion however is inescapable. Although much has been made in the past of the tendency of a majority of Canadians to hold attitudes on many foreign policy issues that are somewhat similar to the attitudes of a majority of Americans, this similarity must be heavily qualified. Not only are Canadians beginning to realize that Canada's "national interests" are somewhat different from those of the U.S. (and this will be explored in part in all of the last five chapters) but the federal government is

[7] See for example, Ronald Sutherland, *Second Image: Comparative Studies in Québec/Canadian Literature* (Toronto, 1971).

aware that symbolic or material attacks from foreign countries on any of the elements of Canadian cohesion must be vigorously discouraged. The Pearson Government's reply to General De Gaulle's "vive le Québec libre" speech in 1967 is probably the most celebrated example. The Trudeau Government's legal and symbolic outputs on the question of Canada's Arctic presence and its use of military forces for territorial (primarily coastal) protection are other examples. The heavy "expressive" concern in the federal government's foreign ownership report on the possible negative results of foreign investment is a partial response to the deeper concern in the 1970's about Canadian "independence." The heavy emphasis given to President Nixon's alleged respect for Canada's "national integrity and independence" in Prime Minister Trudeau's Washington Press Conference on December 7, 1971, is another example.

All of these federal government appeals to those forces or ideas of cohesion that do exist in Canada may strike many foreign observers as evidence of a curious touchiness about Canadian "independence." Yet that is precisely the point. To hold the Canadian condominium together expressive, symbolic, and material actions in external policy may be as important as actions of domestic policy.

Chapter 2

The Provinces: Economic Growth and External Policy

The Trudeau Government's 1970 White Paper on Foreign Policy is the most comprehensive statement of that Government's view of Canada's role in world affairs. It received both blame and praise for its "hard-headed realism," in its explicit enthronement of "economic growth" as the first priority of Canadian external policy. Yet the document nowhere discussed a key set of forces that will inevitably define in practice the types of economic growth Canada will pursue *via* its foreign policy. It did not discuss the nature and tendencies of the provinces' attempts to increase their economic growth. It did not, in short, relate the momentum and content of provincial strategies for economic growth to Canada's external policy. External policy is discussed throughout the White Paper as if it was simply a conjunction of homogenized national priorities with international forces when–especially in the case of Canada–external policy must be an informal blending of national and provincial priorities together with an identification of opportunities and restraints in the external environment. The following is an introductory look at the provincial patterns of economic growth. These patterns amount to key informal influences on federal action in external policy and must be acknowledged.

This said, however, it is no easy task to link these forces clearly to external policy. This short introduction tries simply to suggest a few links by simple exposition; it avoids presentation of statistical tables and aggregate data on provincial economies because the task here is primarily to highlight a few trends and characteristics, not to present a detailed economic report which may or may not suggest relevance to external policy.

BRITISH COLUMBIA

A Montrealer or Torontonian who visits British Columbia (even Vancouver) is struck by the fact that he has left what he might feel is a largely post-industrial environment for an environment which is emphatically industrial (in terms of extractive and other related industry). As an economic unit, British Columbia (2,161,000 population) is heavily dependent on resource extraction both directly and indirectly. Over half of the value of individual output is in four groups of industries: fish packing, wood products, paper products, and primary metals (mainly lead, zinc, and aluminum smelting – industries which involve very little processing). In the rest of Canada, for example, these four industry groups account for less than 25 per cent of total industrial output.[1] Manufacturing industries contribute less to the value – added of the provincial economy (47.8 per cent) compared for example to Ontario (71.9 per cent) and Quebec (67.9 per cent).[2] The major categories of Canada's secondary manufacturing are weakly represented in British Columbia, and the province's large service sector is mainly auxiliary to the resource-centred industries (repair and technical services, transportation, communication, and construction). There are, however, a few sophisticated manufacturing industries such as clothing, musical instruments, electrical equipment, and a Vancouver-based group of firms export engineering services all over the world, especially throughout the Pacific. Tourist services are also significant.

Yet even with an unprecedented dislocation in the provincial economy in 1970, caused by labour-industry confrontations, and the general national economic slump, the basic strength and growing diversity of the province's economy puts it in an enviable economic position for the 1970's. A vigorous mining industry based on copper and coal is gaining in importance in relation to the forest industry. Coal production, for example, rose to 290,000 tons in 1970, from 75,000 tons in 1969.[3] Foreign markets for metals and coal remain strong, particularly in Japan. (Canadian exports to Japan increased 32 per cent in 1970 over 1969, to $793 million.)[4] The province's mineral industry's production rose 7 per cent in 1970.[5] Except for a slump in 1969 the com-

---

[1] Dominion Bureau of Statistics, Ottawa, Canada, (hereafter D.B.S.), *Survey of Production 1969* (Cat. 61-202).
[2] *Ibid.*, pp. 18, 19.
[3] D.B.S., *Canadian Statistical Review* (Oct., 1971), p. 74.
[4] D.B.S., *Trade of Canada: Exports By Country Jan.-Dec. 1970* (Vol. 24, No. 4), p. 185.
[5] See Note 1.

mercial fishing industry has grown steadily.[6] In the same time period, travel receipts rose 10 per cent in 1970; and cash receipts from farm produce rose 3 per cent to $205.8 million.[7]

Wages and incomes in the province are high compared to most of Canada. The average weekly wage and salary (industrial composite) was $147.19 in April 1971 compared to second-place Ontario ($138.10).[8] These wages make British Columbia a magnetic force attracting population. In fact, the provincial government often complains that because it belongs to the federal system it therefore has little control over immigration, or of the influx of people it attracts from the rest of Canada, and this reduces further its *per capita* wealth and increases the services that it must provide such as education, medical care, urban services, welfare, etc. As one of the "have-provinces," B.C. often feels that it is senselessly discriminated against in regional disparity programs. One example is the federal Roads to Resources program of which the Provincial Premier has always complained that the allotment to his province is entirely inadequate. Another example is the Pacific Great Eastern Railway, the third largest in Canada. This was paid for by the province with no operational subsidies from the federal government, while railroads elsewhere in Canada are subsidized (including an American road – the New York Central). British Columbia also complains about the discrimination of freight rates against the West and is anxious to see these rates made more equitable. High costs of transportation both within the province (getting at and removing resources) and from outside have always caused concern.

The province's economic profile frequently conflicts with national tariff policies. To quote Premier W. A. C. Bennett's perhaps overstated summaries:

> Under the national policy of tariffs they (the Eastern industries) have an umbrella over all the markets east and west, and they get that protection and sell their goods everywhere. But B.C. does not get the benefit of selling in the rest of Canada in a protected market. We are on the extreme west. We sell our merchandise . . . on competitive world markets.
>
> (Constitutional Conference Feb. 1968)

[6] D.B.S., *Fisheries Statistics: British Columbia and the Yukon 1969* (Cat. 24-208), May 1971, p. 8.

[7] D.B.S., *Farm Cash Receipts 1970* (Cat. 21-001), Vol. 31, No. 4, p. 6.

[8] D.B.S., *Canadian Statistical Review* (Oct. 1971), p. 50.

And again in December 1969, at the Third Meeting of the Constitutional Conference in Ottawa:

> As far as tariffs are concerned British Columbia depends completely on world trade. Custom tariffs are of no benefit to British Columbia but a tremendous hindrance to our people in the great resource industries – pulp and paper, fishing and lumber and so forth.
>
> They are all penalized by the tariffs in Canada and therefore we say if we pay, if British Columbia pays a fair share of the costs for tariffs, surely if we come to a new constitution we are going to get a share of the revenue returned to the Government of British Columbia.

The commonplace assumptions that this province would flourish under free trade with the U.S. and would benefit if tariffs abroad were lowered may be generally valid, but the argument can be overstated. British Columbia's forest industry exports (except for some crude paper product exports) face generally low tariffs in the U.S. and the U.K. Except for lead and zinc, the same is true for exports of most minerals.[9] The U.S. takes just over half of all B.C. exports, followed by Japan which takes one-fifth, and the U.K. and the European Common Market which take 10 per cent each.[10] Lumber, newsprint, and pulp lead the province's commodity exports, but increases in exports of coal, copper ores and concentrates, and molybdenum are evident. The fishing industry's external restraints are not so much tariffs as international and bilateral fishing agreements, which limit the catch of such major species as halibut and salmon in the North Pacific. Yet it remains true that under free trade the province could no doubt purchase foods and various manufactured goods at reduced prices.

This tension is often recognized by the federal government even though it may remain unresolved (even incrementally). In 1968 Prime Minister Lester Pearson referred to these problems with this example:

> . . . lower wages in Quebec . . . create economic difficulty for a province which has higher wages like British Columbia, lower wages in Hong Kong and Japan create economic difficulties for

---

[9] See R. Shearer *et al, Exploiting Our Economic Potential: Public Policy and the British Columbia Economy* (Toronto: 1968), p. 56-73.

[10] See, *Globe and Mail*, January 22, 1972, p. B3.

Quebec, and if we try to do something about that in a way which prevents the products from Hong Kong and Japan coming into Canada, we will interfere with the high wage products from British Columbia going to Japan and Hong Kong. It is a very complicated problem.

(Federal Provincial Conference, February, 1968)

Another factor controlling provincial development is the extent to which its development is dependent upon federal imagination and co-operation. British Columbia is therefore jealous of its provincial rights in order to lessen its dependence on Ottawa. Federal authority and activity in trade and commerce, banking, control of credit, rail and ship transportation, agriculture, the criminal code, relations with foreign states, world export markets, fisheries, and also electricity, and authority in navigation all add up to an unusually heavy impact on this province because of its resource and export dependence.

ALBERTA

Alberta (1,614,000) is one of the most buoyant economic regions of Canada. It attracts a high proportion of the total investment in the Prairies (over one-half) and although it is heavily dependent on the oil and gas industry it also has a strong agricultural base and its large reserves of coal and timber are also attracting substantial investment. The value-added by the mining industry accounts for 34.1 per cent of all value-added goods-producing industries in the province. This is very high particularly when compared to the national 5 per cent value-added average for the mining industry in Canada's overall goods production (mineral production in Alberta reached $1,-393,503,000 in 1970).[11]

This province is the main source of the crude oil and natural gas for the domestic market (east to the Ottawa river) and for new markets recently opened up in the United States. In fact, existing oil export capacity was fully used in 1971. Expansion of oil and gas pipeline systems in Canada is continuing, and although much of this expansion is outside the province, most of the pipe mill work is being done in Alberta. Also evident is a continuing expansion of gas processing facilities. "In the past year 21 gas-processing plants, valued at $49 million were completed in Alberta and 11 plants, valued at $195

[11] *Ibid.*, and D.B.S., *Preliminary Report on Mineral Production 1970* (Cat. 26-203), October 1971, p. 9.

million were under construction at the end of 1970. An additional 13 plants, to cost $71 million, are proposed." (*Globe and Mail*, January 22, 1971, p. B5.) Alberta also produced 565,000 tons of coal in 1970, 40 per cent of Canada's total production of 1,384,000 tons.[12] This province accounted for 83.6 per cent of all net new production of natural gas in Canada in 1970 and it supplied 75 per cent of all crude oil supplied by Canadian sources in 1970.[13]

Agriculture is of substantial importance to the province and should not be overlooked. Cattle, wheat, and hogs predominate. Farm cash receipts reached $730 million in 1970.[14] Federal incentive grants are helping to encourage manufacturing investment in southern Alberta but most of the province's factory investment is tied either to the oil and gas industries or to agriculture.[15]

SASKATCHEWAN

Saskatchewan (933,000) has always, it seems, been heavily dependent on wheat. It has had difficulties diversifying and finding new markets for its crops but it has tried to push ahead in both directions. Wheat output – mainly because of the federal government's wheat stockpile reduction program – dropped to 8 million acres in 1970 from 16.6 million in 1969, and wheat output fell to 210 million bushels in 1970 from 461 million a year earlier. This decline has been partly offset by increased production of barley, rapeseed, flaxseed, and other field crops. Since foreign sales have increased and major Soviet and Chinese orders were announced in 1971, an increase in wheat production is forecast for the next few years. A major buildup in the cattle and hog population of the province is also helping to diversify Saskatchewan's agricultural base (sales values of cattle was $143 million, hogs $48 million in 1970),[16] yet a sharp buildup in either could, of course, lead to an equally strong decline in prices. Saskatchewan, with the Prairies in general, also suffers from discriminating freight rates which encourage processing of primary crops in Ontario, Quebec, or British Columbia.

Mineral production rose to over $392 million, petroleum to about

[12] See Note 3, p. 74.
[13] See Note 1.
[14] See Note 7.
[15] See the Review of Alberta's economy in the business section of the Toronto *Globe and Mail*, January 22, 1971.
[16] See *Globe and Mail*, January 20, 1971, p. B3, for the statistics in this paragraph

$202.5 million and metals production to $42.3 million in 1970,[17] and these rates of growth provide an important compensation for the disappointment suffered by the too heady assessments of growth in the 1960's for the potash industry. The ten potash mines were operating at less than one-half capacity in 1970 and 1971 because of an over-supply of potash on world markets. Some economists expect that the industry will remain in the doldrums at least until the second half of the 1970's. Despite setbacks, the province has had some success in expanding and preparing to expand its industrial base in the last few years (for example a $50 million uranium mine near Wollaston Lake; a 1000 ton-a-day pulp mill near Meadow Lake, a $6.5 million sawmill near Meadow Lake; a $3 million distillery at Weyburn). The New Democratic Party government in the province has promised to watch the extent to which development of industry and resources involves excessive sell-outs to foreign interests, and this will be a contrast with the performance of the previous government.

MANITOBA

Manitoba (979,000) is Canada's "gateway to the West" and has an astonishingly diverse industrial base, yet appearances can be deceiving. For some time now Manitoba has had to contend with its declining influence as a transportation hub leading to the West. A recent example of this decline is the fact that Air Canada moved its head office and many other facilities to Montreal in the late 1960's. Manitoba does boast an industrial structure "which includes every industrial classification except autos and tobacco" (*Globe and Mail*, January 20, 1971), but it is a province of small, not large, businesses (in 1965, 80 per cent of its firms employed fifty people or less). Some of its efforts to open large and sustaining new enterprises such as the forest products development at The Pas have been plagued by problems.

Food and beverage industries account for over one-third of the province's manufacturing output. The provincial government claims that there are especially attractive opportunities in the food, animal feeds, prefabricated housing, ceiling materials, chemical, and electrical products industries. Mining has been the most expansionary industry in recent years in Manitoba. Cash receipts from farm output is small

[17] See Note 11 and Note 16.

($341.9 million in 1970) compared to Alberta and Saskatchewan, but it is rising slowly.[18]

ONTARIO

Ontario's economy is more diversified than any of the other provinces in Canada and its geographical position is extremely favourable for industrial location with regard to both the domestic market and the important central American markets. The distortions of the tariff barrier are little resented in Ontario; many of Ontario's industries are there because of the tariff (as subsidiaries of foreign, mostly U.S., companies.) Now, however, some economists are beginning to worry about the extent to which the tariff and the branch-plant profile of Ontario has discouraged specialization and product differentiation from the parent. (See the Proceedings of the Ontario Government's Conference on Economic and Cultural Nationalism, August, 1971, and the Science Council of Canada's report on manufacturing industries in October, 1971.)

As one of the richest of the Canadian provinces in terms of income, the province does not depend on federal government development programs. Rather, it subsidizes the less developed regions by way of the federal equalization grants and taxation, providing 45 per cent of the total tax revenues flowing into the national treasury.[19] The response from outside Ontario to its complaints about the tax burden is that Ontario benefits from the tariff which shelters its industry at the expense of the maritime and western provinces which must sell abroad at competitive world prices. Therefore, regional inequities have been used to support arguments for regional and national transportation subsidies, for special assistance to primary producers, for tax concessions, and equalization payments to the lower income provinces. In 1967, Ontario accounted for 52.1 per cent of all wages paid in Canadian manufacturing industries.[20] Canada's *per capita* income

---

[18] See Note 7.
[19] See Economic Council of Canada, *Fifth Annual Review* (Ottawa: 1968) p. 154; and Canadian Tax Foundation, *The National Finances 1970* (Toronto: 1971), for other financial statistics on provincial trades as well as the *Globe and Mail*, May 2, 1970, p. B1.
[20] *Manufacturing Industries of Canada, Section D.* Province of Ontario, 1967 (Feb., 1971), D.B.S., Ottawa, p. 7.

in 1969 was $2913, compared to Ontario's $3368.[21] As Table 3
shows, Ontario dominates a number of Canadian manufacturing industries.

Table 3.   National Importance of Selected Leading Ontario
Manufacturing Industries, 1967[1]

Industry	Per cent of Canada's value of shipments	Rank by value of shipments Ontario	Canada[2]
Iron and steel mills	82.2	2	5
Misc. machinery, equipment	70.5	4	7
Metal stamp., press., coat	63.7	10	12
Misc. metal fabricating	74.3	15	25
Wire and wire products	62.7	20	27
Motor vehicle	89.1	1	1
Motor vehicle parts	97.6	3	9
Aircraft and parts	45.9	16	15
Agricultural implements	76.7	18	32
Communications equipment	60.2	11	13
Electrical indust. equip.	83.2	12	22
Major Appliances	74.4	19	35
Industrial chemicals	60.7	8	11
Commercial printing	57.5	13	16
Publishing and printing	49.7	17	18

[1] I am grateful to Glen Williams of York University for providing this table.
[2] Canada, DBS, *Manufacturing Industries of Canada, Section A, Summary,
1967,* (December, 1970), p. 28.
Source: Ontario Department of Treasury and Economics, *1969 Ontario Statistical Review,* (June, 1970), p. 65.

The Ontario economy remains strong in both the trade and investment sectors.[22] Auto exports to the U.S. were up in 1971. Exports in
crude materials have showed some decline but on the whole Ontario's

[21] Ontario Department of Treasury and Economics, *1969 Ontario Statistical
Review,* June, 1970, pp. 52-3.
[22] In fact, a major academic study suggests Ontario would benefit from free
trade with the U.S. See Paul and Ron Wonnacott, *Free Trade Between the
U.S. and Canada: The Potential Economic Effects* (Cambridge, Mass: 1967).

exports showed an 11 per cent year-to-year increase in the last few years of the sixties. In spite of a softening of steel prices, sales in the steel industry have been strong: for example, sales of pipe for a petroleum pipeline being built by an Oklahoma company, increasing shipments of structural steel to the U.S., and a sale of a considerable volume of rolled steel to fill an order for railway cars for Australia. Ontario Hydro expects further sales of power in both the Canadian and U.S. markets. Overall, the mining industry produces much of the province's Gross Provincial Product (output of $1,631,978,500 in 1970, of which nickel predominates with over $600 million).[23] Investments in Ontario grow every year (up 13.8 per cent in 1970 from 1969), 41 per cent of the increase from 1969 to 1970 was for new construction in the trade, commercial, and financial service sector. Projections for 1971 were for 21 per cent increases in investment in manufacturing, 7 per cent in primary industry, 14 per cent in utilities and 26 per cent in trade, financial, and commercial services.[24]

All this does not leave Ontario without problems. For example, 5.6 per cent of its seasonally adjusted employable work force was without work in September 1971 (see *Globe and Mail*, October 15, 1971, B1). Distribution of development in Ontario is uneven; encouragement of investment has concentrated benefits to the urban areas. (Even the provincial government's much-publicized cancellation in June, 1971, of the Spadina Expressway to the heart of Toronto was followed by commitments for massive funding of a rapid transit and subway system.) Water and sewerage systems, parks, bridges, parking lots, housing, and other services attractive to business location have received funds under the Regional Development Incentives Act while the potential of the northern regions has been neglected. A 1970 report to the regional development branch of the Ontario Department of Treasury and Economics, in noting this "wasteful strategy," suggested a variety of incentives that would assure companies locating in northern Ontario access to the business advantages now available in southern Ontario. Proposed public policies include establishment of pool-warehousing in northern centres for programming improvement of terminal activities, for making funds available for extra costs of warehousing, for sales promotion to sustain non-metropolitan industries, provision of maintenance and technical service operations for branch operations in northern regions, and fuller development of

[23] See Note 11.
[24] See *Globe and Mail*, Jan. 15, 1971, p. B5.

the service sector of the region to diversify work opportunities there. Present industries of the northern area (mainly mining, milling, smelting, and refining operations) lack diversity in their economic base; allied industries such as cement plants, copper and brass mills, and wire cable works should and could be attracted as well.

To meet the needs of northern Ontario, the establishment of a Crown Corporation to develop the area and to build public smelters and pulp mills has been advocated by some political spokesmen who charge that companies at present are not fully and evenly developing the resources of the north. The provincial government has also been criticized for similar failures. These same critics say that the government should reclaim mineral rights and land properties in the name of the public and develop these. Their argument is that twenty-five major mining companies have received exemption of up to ten years from processing in Ontario, and that raw materials only are being sent abroad to Japan, Norway, and the United States. Moreover, much of Ontario's wealth is going to non-resident, foreign-owned corporations. Over 50 per cent of the timber licences in Northern Ontario go to foreign owned companies and much of the profits are invested outside Ontario. It has been suggested that a natural resources tax to give government access to the assets of major corporations could be used to develop areas or communities hit by mine or other industry closures. The concern over foreign, especially American, ownership has a particular edge in Ontario since the province's main interest is in attracting American industries to produce goods that would otherwise have to be imported from the U.S. Former Ontario Premier, John Robarts, admitted this was so and in fact used this argument to counter charges that Ontario was luring industry away from other provinces. Yet the Ontario Government's December 8, 1971, report on foreign ownership breaks from this pattern in its suggestion that Canada's economic sectors be more closely analyzed so that sectors can be identified which need little foreign investment. Although the Ontario Government has been lenient on its resource industries by exempting all the major industries from immediate obligation to undertake more processing, its foreign ownership report calls for a reduction or elimination of "the tax exemptions enjoyed by the oil industry and mining."

QUEBEC

Any introduction to the economy of Quebec (6,023,000, and 80 per cent French-speaking), must begin with a recognition of its severe unemployment problem. Almost 200,000 Quebeckers were looking for work the week before Christmas 1971. Unemployment, seasonally adjusted, reached 9.3 per cent in September, 1971 (*Globe and Mail*, October 15, 1971, B1), and Quebec has close to one-third of all of Canada's jobless. Premier Robert Bourassa campaigned in 1970 on a promise to find 100,000 new jobs for Quebeckers in 1971, and even the most optimistic observers doubted that more than 55,000 could be found. Also, much of this unemployment is middle-class unemployment. This contributes mightily to the alienation of a key part of Quebec's society, forcing it to become less and less receptive to "federalist" claims that separatism is not economically viable. "What have we got to lose" (economically) can be linked with a psychological, political, and cultural drive for *épanouissement*.

Sociological and psychological profiles of Quebec are vital if its position within Confederation is to be understood. At the same time it is useful to recognize here the type of economic activity in which the province engages. Pulp and paper is probably the most important industry in Quebec. There are 56 pulp and paper mills in the province and about 28,450 people work in them with some 16,550 people in the forest, according to *The Globe and Mail*, January 16, 1971, which also reports that: "more than one-third of Canada's pulp output is from Quebec and 45 per cent of the paper and board produced in Canada is produced in Quebec." The higher free-floating Canadian dollar threatens the growth of this industry, yet (in the next few years) it will remain as the largest annual spender for capital expansion in the province.

Quebec produced 13.8 per cent of Canada's minerals[25] in 1970, and most important, 80 per cent of Canada's asbestos.[26] The value of metal mines, asbestos, and some building materials reached $800 million in 1970, and recent contracts with Japanese, West German, British, French, Italian, and Dutch companies by the Iron Ore Company of Canada indicate strong growth in this sector. It is expected sales will be worth a total of about $7 billion in the 1970's. Five Japanese companies are expected to buy $600 million of iron in 15 years.[27]

About 24.4 per cent of Quebec's employed labour force was in manufacturing in 1970, and one-quarter of these were in the clothing, textile, and leather industries.[28] The textile industry is suffering from a

[25] See Note 11.
[26] D.B.S., *Asbestos* (Vol. 440, No. 12, Cat. 26-001), p. 1.
[27] *Globe and Mail*, January 16, 1971, p. B3.
[28] *Ibid.*

decline in production, and it has been pressing Ottawa, with some success, to extend blanket tariff protection. Also, the number of jobs created by federal government subsidization through expansion grants to industry in Quebec has not been able to equal even the amount of layoffs experienced in certain key industrial sectors of the province's economy. A report released by the Quebec Federation of Labour in late 1971 showed that in the six and-a-half months between November 1, 1970, and May 14, 1971, 15,000 Quebeckers were laid off their jobs, and of that total 13,000 layoffs occurred in the industrial sectors being subsidized. These layoffs occurred in the electrical industry, transport materials, textiles and chemical products. Two other major Quebec economic activities – tourism, and shipping – continue to grow. These are bright lights in what has been an otherwise rather dark economic picture in the late 1960's.

Rapid adjustment is needed in the agricultural sector of Quebec's economy. The general militancy of Quebec society has even affected unionized farmers (over half of the commercial farms in Quebec are dairy farms and the dairy industry is under considerable stress because milk is an over-produced commodity in Canada). The Agricultural Minister emphasized that there must be more diversification and modernization, and the changes will be accepted if there is an over-all program to assure decent incomes during the transition. Inefficiency and over-production in agriculture are problems Quebec faces in common with other provinces in Canada.

Three traditional employers of a large work force in Quebec: textiles and the needle trades, furniture, and shoemaking, are in trouble. Now, the new industries which Quebec hopes to attract will be more sophisticated ones that depend on advanced technology, attract highly educated people, and which will hire growing numbers of college graduates. If this is achieved, it will balance the weight of the primary industries (the two biggest are pulp and paper, and mining) and the dying, traditional, industries (such as furniture and shoes). The tourist industry, now third largest in Quebec, continues to show potential, and is being pushed in the hope that it will become a prime revenue producer. The shipping industry is also proving to be a strong contender in producing revenue.

NOVA SCOTIA

Advertisements to businessmen to establish industry in Nova Scotia (pop. 767,000) state that: "Energetic young industry is encouraged to seek production and profit in Nova Scotia. New industry can obtain 100 per cent financing of land and buildings plus 60 per cent financing of installed equipment costs." This sounds enticing to a businessman, but after a number of failures under this scheme the province's industrial promotion agency "Industrial Estates Limited," while stepping up its promotions for industry to locate in Nova Scotia, is becoming much more selective, and so are the federal Economic Expansion and Cape Breton Development programs. By the end of 1970 sixteen industries assisted by IEL had gone out of business but fifty-four remained. The most notable success is the commitment by Michelin Tires Manufacturing Company to build two plants; and the most notable failure is Clairtone Sound Corporation, in which $20 million of provincial funds were invested.[29]

Although this province produces only 1 per cent of Canada's minerals,[30] more emphasis is being placed by IEL on the resource industries, for obvious reasons. An opportunity for a strong petrochemical industry seems realistic, and the forestry industry looks promising even though the province has reached a near deficit situation in its forest resources. (Both improved woodland management and a movement to greater hardwood and low-grade fibre production are apparently needed.) New oil and gas refineries are being constructed and hopes for discoveries of hydrocarbons off the provincial coast together with the advantages of deep water ports for large crude oil tankers also make the province at least cautiously optimistic about important developments in the oil and gas sectors in the seventies. Increasing world demand for coking and thermal coal is tempting the Cape Breton Development Corporation – originally assigned the task of finding alternative work for coal miners – to reassess sources of thermal coal in Cape Breton and to reassess its original mandate. And finally, the unusual success of the deep water container terminals in Halifax has led to plans for another on Bedford; these complement plans for resource development.

Although this province's ideas of the type of economic profile it wishes to emphasize in the seventies are becoming clearer – a profile heavily involved in resource industries – the question still remains as to whether this profile will be sufficiently labour intensive to lessen unemployment, which reached 10.3 per cent in the Maritimes (seasonally adjusted) in September 1971 (*Globe and Mail*, October 15,

[29] *Globe and Mail*, January 13, 1971, p. B5.
[30] See Note 11.

1971, p. B1). To encourage employment, both IEL, DEVCO and the federal regional expansion programs will obviously continue to encourage more processing, manufacturing, and cargo handling in the province. To date, however, dissatisfaction has been expressed by the Atlantic Provinces' Economic Council that the federal DREE program has concentrated on the expenditure of funds for infrastructure without first relating infrastructure to the development of productive enterprises, (see its *Fifth Annual Review* published October, 1971).

NEW BRUNSWICK

In order to reverse the recession of the late sixties in New Brunswick (624,000 pop.) the provincial government hopes to make maximum use of federal regional incentive and other funds to develop the province's potential as a manufacturing service and supply centre with an international orientation. It was announced, November 22, 1971, that Continental Oil is to develop a $60 million, 45 million barrel bulk oil storage depot at Lorneville. In addition, it is hoped a multiple industry complex running from Saint John to Moncton, emphasizing main metal plants and various types of labour-intensive assembly and secondary manufacturing activities, will become a reality. Extractive and primary resource activity in the province has been a mixed success but it is increasing. Major expansions in pulp mills have occurred and more are underway. Provincial mineral output is not buoyant – about $90 million output in 1970,[31] unchanged from 1969 – but there is a possibility of lead-zinc-silver mine developments in the Restigouche and Newcastle areas. Potato shipments are strong and this has pushed farm cash receipts to $57.6 million in 1970.[32] Prices for most species of fish have improved, demand is expected to be strong in the next decade, and this suggests better returns for fishermen and processors in the province.

Yet the problems of high unemployment, migration of the population, and high welfare costs continue to plague New Brunswick and few dramatic improvements on these fronts are expected in the immediate future.

PRINCE EDWARD ISLAND

Canada's tranquil tiny province, Prince Edward Island (110,000), enjoys a strong tourist industry and is cautiously developing more

[31] *Ibid.*
[32] See Note 7.

recreational amenities and motor inns to enhance its valuable natural beauty spots. The caution is characteristic but the commitment to tourism is new. Tourism has displaced fishing as the second major industry behind agriculture, which leans heavily on potatoes, tobacco, and now beef instead of dairy farming. (Net farm cash receipts – $44 million in 1970 – now almost equal New Brunswick's.) The provincial government is also trying to revive the idea of a causeway to the province from New Brunswick by involving American, French, and British private financing as well as the federal government. European structural steel and specialized equipment would be involved in any such project but considerable Canadian content in the form of labour, concrete, and reinforcing steel would be included.[33] If the causeway ever becomes a reality, this would remove Ottawa's less costly obligation to subsidize the current ferry service to the island.

NEWFOUNDLAND

Newfoundland (520,000) may be entering "a new phase of economic development" in the seventies, according to the *Globe and Mail* (January 12, 1971), but it is difficult to see this as anything like a take-off phase. Newfoundland now relies on Ottawa for more than 60 per cent of its government revenues and it has suffered continual setbacks in developing a viable secondary manufacturing sector. Yet, as the *Financial Post* discovered, in an October 23, 1971, review of Newfoundland's economy, the Premier's gradual relinquishment of some of his once almost exclusive power over economic development schemes to a few public servants, allowing them to search for industry, did open up a number of small manufacturing enterprises (approximately 55) in the province in the last few years. Yet large resource-oriented developments were the hallmark of the Smallwood government. Some of these projects which were begun in the late sixties will dominate the development plans of the province in the 1970's as well. These include the 100,000 barrel-a-day oil refinery at Come-By-Chance; a newsprint mill linerboard mill at Stephenville; the extension at Carol Lake by the Iron Ore Company of Canada; and possibilities for a major new hydro development in Labrador. Although these large projects will absorb some labour, they will absorb much capital as well and the extent to which these projects will encourage more labour intensive industry in the long run is not very clear. In contrast the fledgling Newfoundland Development Corporation will emphasize small and medium-sized businesses.

[33] *Globe and Mail*, January 14, 1971, p. B5.

THE NEW RELEVANCE OF PROVINCIAL PRIORITIES TO CANADIAN
EXTERNAL POLICY

How is one to relate these significant, yet in some cases disparate,
provincial trends and biases for economic growth and development to
national schemes for "economic growth"? How much leverage will
these provincial preferences have on the federal government's pursuit
of "economic growth" as its most important priority for external
policy? It is, impossible to answer these questions with any assurance
yet one generalization might be worth consideration.

Not long ago in an analytical discussion of domestic sources of
foreign policy one theorist, James Rosenau, generated a single overall
concluding hypothesis:

> The more an issue encompasses a society's resources and relation-
> ships, the more will it be drawn into the society's domestic political
> system and the less will it be processed through the society's for-
> eign political system.[34]

It is difficult to envisage a foreign policy priority more likely to draw
a society's "domestic political system" into the foreign policy process
than that of the Trudeau Government's first priority which is: "to
increase Canada's economic growth." The momentum of the provinces' economic life therefore has probably never been made more
relevant to Canadian foreign policy. Central to almost all of the
provinces' concerns will be an external policy that does not jeopard-
ize provincial plans for *both* increased resource development and development in other sectors of the economy. The provinces may not
have to worry as much about the consistency of these two demands
compared to the federal government. Both in its domestic programs
(tax, regional economic expansion, and competition policies) and in
its external policies (foreign investment priorities, and trade priorities)
the federal government will be forced to discriminate to some extent
between these two provincial emphases. In addition the federal government is now faced with various international and national economic trends for which provincial governments take very little official
responsibility compared to the federal government. Adverse trends in
the balance and terms of international trade, and foreign control, for
example, will inevitably loom large as influences on Canadian exter-

---

[34] James N. Rosenau "Foreign Policy As An Issue Area," in his edition of
Domestic Sources of Foreign Policy (New York, Free Press: 1967), p. 49.

nal policy and will have to be partially tailored to provincial priorities on economic development. These "national" trends and forces will form part of the discussion in Chapter 4. One significant shift appears to be occurring however that may be pushing provincial economic priorities somewhat closer, than in other decades, to Ottawa's priorities. Except for statements from British Columbia it is clear that all provincial governments are becoming less willing to rely so preponderantly on primary industry development and recognize their growing need for more manufacturing, processing, and service industries for employment purposes. It is significant that after various statements from Ottawa emphasizing the importance of non-resource industries in the wake of President Nixon's surcharge on many Canadian manufactured exports that the Premiers of Alberta, Saskatchewan, Manitoba, and Newfoundland did not object to this so-called "central Canadian" concern but in large measure argued that this concern was becoming theirs as well.[35]

It is necessary first to prevent one misconception that can arise from any economic review of the provincial economic profiles in Canada. The strain on the political system in Quebec cannot be understood solely by reference to economic parameters. The following chapter will therefore take a sustained look at the nature and causes of political and social stress in Quebec. Although the implications of the Quebec problem for external policy are not as obvious as the problems discussed in this chapter, this problem, which is probably the most explosive and intractable in the Canadian condominium, could end up affecting Canadian external policy simply because the political support to any federal government is now under question in Quebec.

---

[35] See the series of articles on this by Peter Desbarats in the *Toronto Star* during November 1971, and the comments by Newfoundland's Premier before the election in his province as reported in the *Financial Post*, October 23, 1971.

Chapter 3

Quebec: Canada's Special Challenge and Stimulus

Before moving to a discussion of Canada's nation-wide problems of economic growth and their relevance to external policy, it is vital to describe one more essential feature of the Canadian condominium which has relevance for overall political integration and economic stability: the unique strains in the province of Quebec. Here we must move from the economic parameters somewhat and concentrate on dominant trends in the political life of contemporary Quebec. In many ways the whole nature of Canada cannot be grasped without understanding this province. This chapter is guided by the general observation that polity and society are closely interrelated, as in the condominium concept. Major changes in one induce major changes in the other. The direction and extent of this exchange will vary with time and place, but the general relationship will almost always obtain.

In the case of Quebec, we know that society there has undergone profound change over recent decades. Thus, we have good reason to suspect that the dynamism of political life in contemporary Quebec can be properly understood only after we have first examined this societal transformation and have sought to trace its possible impact upon political life. The process of social change was initiated by urbanization and industrialization. These forces in turn induced, in particular, a multiplication of élites, an intensification of ethnic interaction and conflict, and a profound reorientation of the educational system. Moreover, this reorganization of French-Canadian society has been conditioned by Anglophone control of the industrial economy.

The impact upon the political system of this social change can be clearly seen in terms of two dominant trends in Quebec political life: an increasing heterogeneity and conflict of political belief systems, and a pluralization and intense opposition among political parties, interest groups, etc. In the process, the Quebec political system has become increasingly marked by a profound uncertainty about the direction of its future development. This condition puts the province on the threshold of two basic challenges which may well determine this future development: the continuing struggle to introduce all Quebecois into a satisfactory role within the technological society and the struggle to ensure that Quebec will be animated by an autonomous Francophone culture.[1]

THE QUEBEC SOCIAL SYSTEM: THE DIMENSIONS OF CHANGE

Until the beginning of this century, French Canada could still be described as an essentially traditional society. It was primarily rural (in 1891 Quebec's population was 71.1 per cent rural[2]), the bulk of its population being distributed among small parish units which were the focal points for most activity. For most of this rural population, economic activity was centred upon small, self-sufficient, family farms. In short, the base of French-Canadian society was highly decentralized; most French Canadians tending to identify with their locality rather than with the French-Canadian society in Quebec as a whole.[3] As for the élites (both rural and urban), they were concentrated primarily among professions which serviced the traditional society, such as the clergy, and liberal professions of medicine and law. Paralleling this social structure, the educational system was geared primarily to the preparation of candidates for these traditional élite careers. Among the rural masses the level of education was low.

[1] This chapter will seek to construct a general framework for the analysis of political life in Quebec – delineating the major directions of social and political change. At times, statements will be presented about specific relationships among these different variables. But many of these statements cannot be fully tested on the basis of available information and should be treated as mere hypotheses. Also, it should be borne in mind that, given the limited space available, this chapter is restricted to characterizing mere patterns and trends. In many cases, it is not possible to elaborate points beyond a bare minimum; nor is it always possible to introduce appropriate qualifications and nuances.
[2] Calculated from *1901 Census of Canada*, Volume 1 (Ottawa: Queen's Printer), p. 20.
[3] See Marcel Rioux, "Conscience éthnique et conscience de classe au Québec," *Recherches sociographiques*, VI, I, 1965, p. 30.

A crucial consequence of this kind of social organization was that it encouraged little contact with Anglo-Saxons. The rural parishes, which encompassed the daily life of most inhabitants, were invariably completely French-Canadian. As for the élites, their concentration upon services for the traditional society freed most of them from conflict with Anglo-Saxon competitors. To the extent that these rural and élite structures could accommodate all the French-Canadian population (significantly, this was never completely the case), ethnic contact, and especially ethnic competition, could be avoided. By the same token, this relative autonomy of the French-Canadian social system meant that most French Canadians could meet their needs in the French language. It was in this form that French Canada had survived conquest by the British.

By the turn of the century, this traditional pattern was being undermined by urbanization. By 1921, Quebec's population was for the first time more urban than rural. This process has continued; by 1961 Quebec's population was 74.9 per cent urban.[4] Thus, French-Canadian society has long lost its rural base. In fact it lost it faster and more completely than even Ontario. This rapid urbanization was paralleled by industrialization. By 1961, French Canada had long ceased to be an agrarian society – only 9.0 per cent of Quebec's adult male work force was still engaged in agriculture.[5] Today the population of the province is over 80 per cent urban and the work force is even more heavily engaged in non-agricultural work.[6]

[4] In 1921 the Quebec population was 51.0 per cent urban; in 1961 it was 74.9 per cent urban. "General Review: Rural and Urban Population," *1961 Census of Canada*, Bulletin 71-2 (Ottawa: Dominion Bureau of Statistics), p. 2-24. In 1921, "the urban population was defined as the population residing in incorporated cities, towns and villages, while the remainder was treated as rural" (*ibid.*, p. 2-1). In 1961, "all cities, towns and villages of 1,000 and over whether incorporated or not, were classed as urban, as well as the urbanized fringes of (a) cities classed as metropolitan areas, (b) those classed as other major urban areas, and (c) certain smaller cities, if the city together with its urbanized fringe was 10,000 population or over. The remainder of the population was classed as rural." *Ibid.*, Bulletin 11-7, *Introduction*. The 1961 method of classification was also the basis of the 1966 data cited below.

[5] *Ibid.*, "General Review: The Canadian Labour Force," Bulletin 7, pp. 1-12, 12-22.

[6] The results of the 1971 census were not available at the time of writing. However, we do know that between 1961 and 1966, the urban proportion had already risen from 74.9 per cent to 78.3 per cent. This second figure was calculated from "Population: Rural and Urban Distribution," *1966 Census of Canada*, Catalogue 92-608, Volume 1, 1-8 (Ottawa: Dominion Bureau of Statistics, March, 1968), p. 13-3. We can assume that over the period 1966-1971, the urban population continued to increase – at least at a rate sufficient to reach the 80 per cent mark.

Nevertheless, it should be kept in mind that in two respects French Canada has not fully completed the conversion to a modern industrial society. First of all, a significant segment of the population (close to 20 per cent) continues to live outside the urban centres. Consequently, traditional values and structures maintain a more solid base in French-Canadian society than is sometime realized. The inevitable conflict between this rural minority and the more urban majority is exacerbated by the fact that rural Quebec, disadvantaged by the direction of economic development, is undergoing increasing economic and social strain.[7]

The conversion of French Canada to an industrial society is also incomplete in another and much more critical sense. While the bulk of French Canadians now participate, in some way, in an industrial economic system, this system is not directly controlled within French-Canadian society; French Canadians neither own the corporate structures nor, to any significant sense, manage them.

The industrialization of Quebec was carried out almost entirely by non-French Canadians. These "étrangers" were actively encouraged by a series of provincial governments which, despite the agrarian tenets of the dominant nationalist ideology, treated industrialization, *per se*, as a progressive measure. Generally, these governments accepted that the industrialization process be financed and directed by English Canadians and Americans. French-Canadian participation was usually restricted to the lower ranks of the industrial hierarchy. This general pattern has persisted to the present day, as is clearly demonstrated by recent studies for the Royal Commission on Bilingualism and Biculturalism.[8] (As one might expect, given the sources of industrialization in Quebec, the Quebec economy has become highly dependent upon markets in Ontario and the United States.) Quebec's resource-based sectors are dependent on sales to the U.S. (65 per cent of its international exports go to the U.S.) and its conventional industries are dependent on Ontario sales (60 per cent of its exports within Canada go to Ontario).[9]

In economic terms, then, French-Canadian society can be seen as a "partial society," that is to say, its institutions do not encompass

---

[7] The nature of this strain and its relationship to support for the Social Credit Party are analysed in Maurice Pinard, *The Rise of a Third Party: A Study in Crisis Politics* (Englewood Cliffs, N.J.: Prentice-Hall, 1971).

[8] See the *Report of the Royal Commission on Bilingualism and Biculturalism, Book III: The Work World* (Ottawa: Queen's Printer, 1969), Part 1: "Socio-economic status and ethnic origin."

[9] *Financial Post*, December 19, 1970.

major economic activities. This same condition is, to a less pronounced degree, experienced in English Canada as well. Nevertheless, turning to the political implications of such conditions, it is important to see that the issue of economic control has the potential for dividing as well as uniting the political allegiances of English and French Canadians. With respect to ownership of economic enterprises, English Canada and French Canada share a similar relationship to the United States. In both English Canada and Quebec a substantial proportion of economic enterprises are American-owned.[10] This, then could provide a rationale for the use of common political structures. One might argue that common political structures would afford a more effective counter to American ownership and its effects, than would the separate efforts of distinct political structures. However, this possible economic incentive for close political collaboration is endangered by the fact that ownership within the Quebec economy resides, not merely with Americans, but to a significant degree with English Canadians.[11] This situation could induce French Canadians to conclude that the political interests of French Canada and English Canada are, in fact, as fundamentally opposed as are those of French Canada and the United States. This second possibility is very much strengthened by the fact that, whatever the locus of ownership of Quebec economic structures, the management positions within these structures are primarily held, not by Americans, but by English Canadians. Thus, it is English Canada which might be perceived as the immediate obstacle to a greater French-Canadian role in the Quebec economy.

As one might expect, the weakness of the French-Canadian role in the creation of an industrial economy in Quebec is reflected in the other major changes that French-Canadian society has undergone over recent decades – changes that have, for the most part, resulted from the dictates of the industrial economy.

[10] The Royal Commission on Bilingualism and Biculturalism found that (in 1961) in the manufacturing sector of the Quebec economy, 31.3 per cent of the labour force worked for "foreign-owned" establishments; in the mining sector 40.4 per cent of the work force worked for such establishments, *Report of the Royal Commission, Book III: The Work World*, p. 54. Presumably, the vast majority of these "foreign-owned" establishments were American-owned.
[11] According to the Commission, in 1961, 37.7 per cent of the total Quebec labour force worked for establishments owned by "Anglophone Canadians." Within the manufacturing industry establishments owned by Anglophone Canadians represented 42.8 per cent of the "total value added." The comparable figure for establishments owned by Francophone Canadians was 15.4 per cent, (*ibid.*, pp. 54-56.).

One of the most spectacular of these changes has been the pluralization of the élite structure. While the élite of traditional French Canada were involved in several different occupations (and there was always some feuding among them over power and status), they were united by the fact that their positions all depended upon the particular needs and values of a traditional agrarian society. With the development of an urban, industrial Quebec, not only were these élites increasingly ill-equipped to administer to the needs of French Canadians, but new French-Canadian élites arose that were oriented to servicing the needs of this new segment of the society. They tended to have world-views and interests that challenged those of the traditional élites.

Significantly, when an administrative élite developed in French Canada, it developed outside the Anglophone-dominated industrial structure.[12] This élite appeared within the various social and economic organizations that the clergy had to develop in an effort to serve its flock within the new urban milieu. Eventually, it was able to wrest control of these structures from the Church. Thus, hospitals, educational institutions, welfare agencies, etc., came under lay control, and the popular influence of the clerical élite steadily declined. Similarly, this administrative élite has steadily eroded the control that members of the traditional liberal professions had long been able to exercise over the governmental apparatus.

Paralleling this rise of an administrative élite has been the rise of various élites whose power and influence is based directly upon urban occupational organizations such as trade unions, teacher associations and, to some extent, upon lower class protest movements such as the *groupes des citoyens*. Increasingly, these élites are attacking the "technocratic" power of the administrative élite.[13]

[12] This argument is especially well-developed in writings of Hubert Guindon. In particular, see Hubert Guindon, "The Social Evolution of Quebec Reconsidered," *The Canadian Journal of Economics and Political Science*, XXVI (November, 1960), pp. 533-51, reprinted in Marcel Rioux and Yves Martin, ed., *French-Canadian Society*, Vol. 1 (Toronto: McClelland and Stewart, 1964), pp. 137-161; and Hubert Guindon, "Two Cultures: An Essay on Nationalism, Class and Ethnic Tension," ed. Richard H. Leach, *Contemporary Canada* (Durham, N.C.: Duke University Press, 1967), pp. 33-59. Other themes of this chapter can also be found in these two outstanding essays.

[13] For a revealing case study of challenge to established élites in a rural setting see the articles on *Opération Dignité* in *Le Devoir*, August 13, 14, and 15, 1971. The *Opération Dignité* movement has sought to mobilize Eastern Quebec residents on behalf of local projects for economic development and social improvement. In doing so, it has directly challenged both traditional political élites and administrative élites.

Thus, unlike traditional French Canada, contemporary French Canada has several distinct élite groups, each with its own base of support and its distinctive interest and world-view. Much of the dynamism in the life of contemporary Quebec can be seen as a struggle among these élites. Nevertheless, reflecting the Anglophone domination of the Quebec economy, these new élites developed either within the lower reaches of the economic structures or outside these structures altogether. French Canada has yet to acquire a major economic élite.

Another major consequence of the industrialization of Quebec has been an intensification of contact between French Canadians and English Canadians. Accelerated urbanization has increased the geographical proximity of English and French Canadians in Quebec, most especially in Montreal. Direct contact is generally restricted, however, to the work world. Here it is structured by the Anglophone domination of the economy: in much of the work world French Canadians are subordinate to English Canadians. Accordingly, in this one area of interaction between the two ethnic groups there is a strong possibility that French Canadians will find the interaction unsatisfactory. This will be especially likely if the French Canadians perceive that their advancement within the economic structure is blocked by the Anglophones who control these structures.

The difficulties of English-French relations within the work world are further compounded by the fact that, reflecting the concentration of economic power among Anglophones, the Quebec work world tends, at least at the higher levels, to operate in English. This means, of course, that French Canadians, most of whom have been educated entirely within a French language educational system, may be considerably handicapped in performing their jobs and in securing promotion (at the same time, to the extent that French Canadians do succeed in performing their work in English, working in this second language may undermine their ability to use French in other contexts). This dimension of social change, the failure of economic structures to allow French-speaking Quebecois to work in the French language at all levels, poses a major challenge to French-Canadian society in Quebec.[14]

Additionally, there is at least some evidence to suggest that Eng-

[14] See *Report of the Royal Commission on Bilingualism and Biculturalism, Book III: The Work World*, Part 3, "The Private Sector," (Ottawa: Queen's Printer, 1969).

lish-French relations within the work world are complicated by differences in the values and norms that guide performance in the work world.[15] These differences may disappear quite readily through participation in common structures. But until this occurs, these differences can provide a further source of ethnic friction and could be used as an additional basis for discrimination against French Canadians.

It should be borne in mind that the incidence of linguistic and cultural strain would be largely independent of the citizenship of the Anglophones involved – it could be experienced with English Canadians just as easily as with Americans. Thus, to the extent this strain affects political allegiances, it would encourage an attachment to Quebec rather than collaboration with English Canadians in efforts to counter American influence.

A final major effect of industrialization in Quebec has been to induce a rapid reorientation of the French-Canadian educational system. A system that in the past had concerned itself primarily with the classical training of a small traditional élite has now been charged with the responsibility of educating the mass of French Canadians so that they can participate more fully in the technological society. This has involved a radical transformation of structures and the introduction to higher levels of a much greater part of French-Canadian youth. As a consequence of the success of these efforts, contemporary French-Canadian society is characterized by a singularly large gap between the levels of education of its youth and its adults. This has served to create a profound divergence in the world-views of the two generations and to upset the previous authority relationships between the generations.[16]

In addition to this internal change within French-Canadian society, reorientation of the educational system has, through its effect on occupational aspirations, served to heighten greatly the ethnic tensions stemming from Anglophone domination of the Quebec economy. To find the positions of administrative and technical responsibility to which they aspire, graduates of this new educational system must, for

[15] See the unpublished study of G. A. Auclair and W. H. Read, "A Cross-cultural Study of Industrial Leadership," prepared for the B and B Commission. The results of this study are briefly described in *Report of the Royal Commission on Bilingualism and Biculturalism, Book III: The Work World*, Part 3, "The Private Sector," (Ottawa: Queen's Printer, 1969), pp. 480-482.

[16] The principal treatment of this phenomenon is Jacques Lazure's *La Jeunesse du Québec en révolution: essai d'interprétation* (Montréal: Les Presses de l'Université du Québec, 1970). The book is limited primarily to the elaboration of hypotheses.

the large part, look to the economic system. Thus, although educated in French, they must compete with Anglophones for positions in a system that is dominated by the English language. Moreover, according to some studies, this system has tended to discriminate against French Canadians at the higher levels.[17] Accordingly, Quebec political life has been increasingly coloured by an apprehension that the aspirations of large numbers of young Francophones – aspirations resulting from a transformed educational system – cannot be satisfactorily met within Quebec's economic system as it is presently structured.

In sum, over recent decades French Canada has been induced, primarily by external forces, to change from a predominantly traditional society to a predominantly technological society. Thus the way of life of most of the masses of French Canada has been radically altered, and new élites have arisen to contest the leadership of traditional élites. These processes have engendered disorientation and strain. But what is even more capable of inducing stress is the fact that in two respects this transformation to a technological society is not complete. As in any contemporary industrialized society, traditional structures and mentalities do continue to retain some support, especially in rural areas. But more importantly, the economic system in which most French Canadians now participate is neither owned nor directed by French Canadians. It has continued to be dominated by Anglophones. Thus, French Canada's recently pluralized élite structures still lack a major economic élite and its new technology-oriented educational system is preparing many young French Canadians for careers that, to a significant degree, either may not really be open to them, or may involve a high degree of linguistic strain and ethnic tension. This failure of Quebec's economic structures to meet the needs and aspirations of French Canadians poses the gravest of all challenges to French-Canadian society in Quebec.

THE QUEBEC POLITICAL SYSTEM: THE IMPACT OF SOCIAL CHANGE

The impact that this reorganization of French-Canadian society has had upon the Quebec political system can be discerned by examining two central aspects of political life: belief systems and political structures.

---

[17] Apparently, such a conclusion is presented in an unpublished research report submitted to the B and B Commission by André Raynauld and Gerald Marion. See the discussion on the contents of this report in Gilles Racine, "Les Québécois gagnent peu à cause de la ségrégation économique pratiquée par les anglophones à leur endroit," *La Presse*, 14 novembre, 1970.

Political Belief Systems: From Consensus to Conflict

The response of political belief systems to social change can be traced to three basic components: the definition of the nature of French-Canadian society, the role of government, and the nature of authority.

Throughout the nineteenth century and into the present century, the dominant belief system saw French Canada as necessarily an agrarian society.[18] It was generally affirmed that only in this form could French Canada maintain sufficient autonomy and coherency to fulfill its historic mission: to preserve a French and Catholic civilization in North America. As an agrarian society, French Canada could minimize contact with the English, thus preserving its French character. Moreover, the agrarian way of life, with the parish as its central unit, was best suited to the practice of Catholicism. Thus the emphasis was upon preventing change, maintaining a continuity with the past. Perhaps reflecting the fact that industrialization was introduced to Quebec by non-French Canadians, this image of French Canada, best expressed in the motto *Je me souviens*, was affirmed long after Quebec had ceased to be predominantly rural and agrarian.[19]

By the 1950's, however, this image of French Canada was under heavy attack and began to yield to a new formulation. By this time urbanization and industrialization had become too pervasive for the traditional image to be a credible representation of French-Canadian society. The bulk of the population was preoccupied with problems that could not be recognized within the traditional perspective. Moreover, the new bureaucratic élite, which was rapidly rising to power, was championing a new and more credible image of French-Canadian society.

[18] The agrarian model of society appears to have been central to the political beliefs of the bulk of French Canada's élites. The ideal appears to have played a significant role in guiding élite behaviour, as well as merely legitimizing it. However, there are grounds for suspecting that the agrarian ideal never had the same centrality in the political beliefs of the masses of French Canada. Certainly, the history of massive emigrations to urban centres – dating back to the latter half of the nineteenth century when New England was the main destination – indicates that the masses were not constrained by a moral commitment to agrarianism.

[19] This belief system is well documented in Michel Brunet's critical study, "Trois dominates de la pensée canadienne-française: l'agriculturisme, l'antiétatisme et le messianisme," in Michel Brunet, *La Présence anglaise et les Canadiens: Etudes sur l'histoire et la pensée des deux Canadas* (Montréal: Beauchemin, 1958), pp. 113-166. A useful collection of statements of these beliefs is Ramsay Cook, ed., *French-Canadian Nationalism: An Anthology* (Toronto: Macmillan, 1969).

Within this new perspective, French Canada was irrevocably launched on the path of industrialization and technological change and, in fact, it was in this direction that it was to achieve its new destiny. Thus, the basic thrust, it was argued, had to be an intensification of this movement. The credo became one of *rattrapage* (catching up), essentially to the North American model. *La survivance* was replaced with the more positive *l'épanouissement*. The mission of French Canada became a secular mission – to create a modern technological society animated by a French spirit. Implicit in such a goal is greater French-Canadian control of the economy of Quebec.[20]

More recently, with the consolidation of working-class organizations and the increasing prominence of the leadership of these organizations, this second image of French-Canadian society has been challenged by yet a third. Accusing the former of projecting the needs and aspirations of primarily the new bureaucratic middle class, this perspective stresses that the bulk of French Canadians are members of the working class. It argues that the over-riding goal of French Canada now must be the redistribution of economic and social benefits in favour of this segment of the society, as well as the transformation of political structures to facilitate mass participation in legislative and administrative decision-making. Increasingly, the argument is being made that French Canada's natural development lies, not in the imitation of the dominant North American model of society, but in the construction of a truly socialist society.[21] Just as the themes of *rattrapage* and *révolution tranquille* dominated much of Quebec pol-

[20] For provocative analyses of this perspective see Léon Dion, "Genèse et caractères du nationalisme de croissance," Congrès des Affaires canadiennes, *Les Nouveaux Québécois* (Québec: Les Presses de l'Université Laval, 1964), pp. 59-76; Gérard Bergeron, *Le Canada-francais: après deux siècles de patience* (Paris: Editions du Seuil, 1967), Chapter VI; and Jean-Marc Leger, "Paradoxes d'une revolution ou le temps des illusions," Fernand Dumont and Jean-Paul Montiminy, eds., *Le pouvoir dans la societé canadienne-francaise* (Québec: Les Presses de l'Université Laval, 1966), pp. 36-38.

[21] This working-class populism is articulated, within a revolutionary perspective, in the remarkable "autobiography" of Pierre Vallières, *Nègres blancs d'amerique: Autobiographie précoce d'un terroriste québécois* (Nouvelle edition revue et corrigée, Montréal: Editions parti pris, 1969). Within the context of this present discussion, the book is especially striking for its bitter attack on the upper classes of French-Canadian society. Thus, while there is a clear commitment to political independence for Quebec, this independence is seen as only the first stage in the seizure of power by the Quebec working class – the "national revolution" must be followed by a "social revolution" in which the targets will be essentially French Canadian. For more theoretical elaborations of this perspective see the two periodicals: *Parti Pris* and *Socialisme Québécois*. A useful collection of *Parti Pris* statements is *Parti Pris, Les Québécois* (Paris: Maspero, 1967).

itical life during the 1960's, a working-class populism may be very much in evidence in the 1970's. Within this perspective as well, French-Canadian control of the Quebec economy becomes imperative, with the added condition that this control should be exercised directly by the working class of French Canada.

A continuing redefinition of the nature of French-Canadian society has been paralleled by a similar process concerning the role of government. Traditionally, this role was defined in highly restricted terms. In a rural, agrarian society, the material needs of most of the population were derived from the family farm. Thus, dependence upon governmental services was minimal. Moreover, French Canadian élites argued, with Catholicism as a central characteristic of the society the church had a pre-eminent role to play (the Church was not alone in making this argument), a pre-eminence to which the state must subordinate its own activities. Whatever material needs could not be satisfied through the family farm should and would be administered by the Church. On this basis then, government had little positive role to play in French-Canadian society. Accordingly, the main concern about government was that it should not take actions which might harm that society.

With such little positive value attached to government, it was not too difficult to find satisfactory terms for Quebec participation in a Canadian political system. The essential aspect of governmental activity was not the benefit it might bring to French Canada – this was seen as marginal – but the damage which, if in the wrong hands, governmental action might do to French Canada. Thus, as long as French Canada was protected from hostile governmental action in key areas – of which education was central – then most of its interests were accommodated. This could be accomplished by assigning these responsibilities to a Quebec provincial government, controlled by a primarily French-Canadian electorate. Within this perspective, then, the essential role of the Quebec government was to prevent undesirable activity by other governments rather than to be an active agent in its own right. In fact, the most important of these jurisdictions which the Quebec government was to retain – education – was, in practice, administered not by Quebec but by the Church. In time, French-Canadian élites became increasingly suspicious of the federal government, both because of decisions made within federal jurisdictions and because of alleged federal intrusions in provincial jurisdictions. Thus even greater importance was attached to the Quebec government's value as a guardian against actions harmful to French-Canadian interests. But the general theory of the place of government in French-Canadian society, including that of the government of Quebec, remained essentially unchanged.

However, this restrictive theory was displaced as the image of French Canada as an industrial society gained increasing dominance. French-Canadian society was now in desperate need of an active government devoted to it alone. The state was seen to be the only agent capable of the *rattrapage* of French-Canadian society. It now had to assume full responsibility for both education and welfare. Accordingly, when the new bureaucratic élite acceded to political power in the 1960's, the old federal arrangement was no longer acceptable. It did not assign to the government of Quebec all the various powers that it required in order to be the *moteur principal* of French Canada's *l'épanouissement*. This attack on the federal structure was reinforced by an increasing dissatisfaction with the extent and conditions of French-Canadian participation in the economy. French Canadians doubted whether they would be permitted to rise within the Anglo-Saxon-dominated structures. They reasoned that if they were to obtain control of the Quebec economy – to be *maîtres chez nous* – the Quebec government would have to be the primary agent, and would need greatly increased powers. Finally, it could be argued that increased ethnic tension served directly to undermine the very principle of sharing a political system with English Canadians. Instead, it was felt, the symbols of government should be exclusively French Canadian – or, more precisely, *québecois*.

The new working-class populism also reflects the need for a changed government role, one which is geared to meet the pressing economic and social needs of the urban French-Canadian working class. Moreover, it is usually alleged, a Quebec government freed from domination by the federal government and Anglo-Saxon corporations would be best able to pursue this role. With the rise of new élites presenting a new image of French Canada, the federal arrangement is again put into question.

A third direction which traces the impact of social change upon political belief systems concerns definitions of the nature of authority. In traditional French Canada both polity and society appear to have been permeated by a conception of authority that was hierarchical. Authority resided, not in the people, but in some particular élite. In the case of the Church, authority resided in the clerical élites, who received it from God. As for political authority, it necessarily was

held by the established governmental structures which, in turn, derived their authority from a monarch or God. In either case, the
obligation of the masses was to accept the rulings handed down to
them.[22]

The appearance and acceptance of new theories of authority that
were not hierarchical in nature seem to be closely related to the transformation of French-Canadian society. The new bureaucratic élites
directly challenged the authority of the church in many ° :as of social
and political life and generally stressed liberal democratic values.
Working-class élites are presenting an essentially populist conception
of authority. The reorientation of the educational system has also contributed to the rejection of the traditional conception of authority.
First, it popularized liberal democratic values – as symbolized by the
collège d'enseignement général et professionnel (CEGEP) which combines all educational streams. More importantly perhaps, by educating
the bulk of French-Canadian youth to a much higher level than that
obtained among older French Canadians, the system has dramatically
upset the previous relationship between generations. Because of the
level of education achieved, young French Canadians do not seem to
feel great deference to the older generation – especially true, it seems, in
the case of working-class families. This has had the effect of apparently
freeing many French-Canadian young people from any sense of obligation to accept without question established authority structures.

At present in Quebec, there appears to be no dominant theory of
authority. Among the competing new formulations, however, there
does appear to be a universal rejection of the previously affirmed
obligation to obey without question established governmental structures. Quebec political life seems to be pervaded by a spirit of *revendi-
cation*, demanding that government respect its obligation to a particular group. As the FLQ showed in October, 1970, and before, there is
now support even for the argument that violence is justified when a
group's rights are not fully recognized by governments.

By examining three central components of the political belief systems of French Canada, it can be seen that social change has had a
profound impact upon the polity. In response to social change, each
of these central components has undergone reformulation. It should

[22] These themes are developed by Pierre Elliott Trudeau, "Some Obstacles to
Democracy in Quebec," in Pierre Elliott Trudeau, *Federalism and the French
Canadians* (Toronto: Macmillan, 1968), pp. 103-123; and in Camille Laurin,
"Autorité et personnalité au Canada français," in Camille Laurin, *Ma traversée
du Québec* (Montreal: Les Editions du Jour, 1970).

be kept in mind, however, that in none of these cases has the new formulation completely supplanted the former. Rather than a complete transformation of beliefs, social change appears merely to have engendered antitheses. The contemporary condition is a new heterogeneity and tension among beliefs rather than the conversion to a new homogeneity.[23] Thus, with respect to the nature of French-Canadian society, substantial segments of the population continue to believe that, while perhaps not essentially agrarian, French Canada is by nature Catholic and that the Church should continue to have pre-eminence within many areas of society. As was demonstrated during the 1966 provincial election, many rural French Canadians regard education as an example of Church pre-eminence in one area. They were very disturbed by the role that the state was assuming in education, at the expense of the Church. Similarly, regarding the role of government, a substantial segment of the population continue to resist the contention that government must be responsible only to French-Canadian society, that French Canada cannot afford to share governmental structures with English Canada. This resistance is most forcefully articulated by a generation of intellectuals, profoundly marked by its battles with Quebec Premier Duplessis' regime, especially from 1950 to 1959. For this group, which includes Pierre Trudeau, Jean Marchand and Gérard Pelletier, an entirely separate French-Canadian polity is highly undesirable since it would necessarily support an intense nationalism which could be inherently reactionary. Also, a pragmatic and thus perhaps less stable basis for resisting the idea of an entirely French-Canadian polity has been presented by Liberal Premier Robert Bourassa and his regime. According to this approach, French Canada can meet its own needs while sharing its polity with English Canada. Moreover, according to this group, any attempt to restructure the polity in a separatist way could have disastrous economic effects. Both these positions are strongly entrenched in particular segments of French-Canadian society.

Finally, there continue to be many in Quebec who are prepared to accept authority without equivocation and who regard the rest of society as being obligated to behave similarly. The strength of this sentiment was demonstrated by the large popular support for former Quebec Attorney-General Claude Wagner and his appeals to "law

---

[23] This argument is very well elaborated in Léon Dion, "La polarité des idéologies: conservatisme et progressisme," Dumont and Montminy, OPCH, pp. 23-25.

and order."[24] Similarly, Réal Caouette may have been expressing the opinion of a significant segment of the French-Canadian population when after the murder of Pierre Laporte, he declared that the FLQ members presently held in custody should be summarily executed.[25]

In sum, the effect of social change on political belief systems has been the creation of an enduring plurality, each element rooted in a segment of the society. Moreover, this plurality extends to fundamental values. As a consequence, Quebec political life is pervaded by a profound uncertainty and uneasiness. At a time when the survival of French Canada is more in question than perhaps ever before there is no clear consensus about the appropriate goals and strategy.

As one might expect, this plurality of values within Quebec is reflected in a conflict within English-Canadian public opinion over the nature of the goals of Quebec and the possibility of accommodating these goals within a Canadian framework. One position, strongly entrenched within the leadership of the Liberal Party, operates from an opposition to all forms of nationalism. It contends that the political demands of the majority of French Canadians are essentially unrelated to the aspirations of Quebec nationalists and can be accommodated within a federal framework approximating that which cur-

[24] In a survey published in July, 1969, it was shown that Claude Wagner would draw the greatest support for the Liberal Party if he were its leader. He was shown to be more popular than the other possible contenders for the party leadership, as well as the current party leader – Jean Lesage. This popularity was interpreted, in an accompanying article, as a function of Wagner's association with "law and order," See "C'est Wagner contre Lesage," *Le Magazine Maclean*, juillet, 1969, pp. 19-22.

[25] This declaration is cited in John Saywell, *Quebec 70: A Documentary Narrative* (Toronto: University of Toronto Press, 1971), p. 107.

With respect to the War Measures Act imposed during the October crisis, most French Canadians appear to have been in approval. Thus, a survey made among Quebec French Canadians in November, 1970, showed that 72.8 per cent of the persons interviewed thought the War Measures Act was justified; 15.6 per cent thought it was unjustified, and 11.6 per cent were undecided. (*La Presse*, 28 novembre, 1970.)

Nevertheless, there are indications that the judgment has since become less favourable. A survey administered in May, 1971, indicated a much more mixed attitude toward the governmental handling of the October Crisis. Only a minority of the Francophone population of Quebec was fully in support of the governmental measures. (When asked whether they approved the conduct of the Bourassa government during the October events, 36.5 per cent of the French-Canadian respondents were entirely in approval, 33.6 per cent were in only partial approval, 20.1 per cent were in total disapproval, and 9.8 per cent did not have an opinion or would not respond. Michel Bellavance et Marcel Gilbert, "La crise d'octobre et l'opinion publique au Québec," *Le Devoir*, 29 mai, 1971.)

ently exists. This position, and the visibility it received through its endorsement by the government leadership, has helped to eliminate from current discussion proposals that would give special powers to Quebec while retaining most of the present framework.

On the other hand, there also has developed within English Canada an increasingly strong nationalist sentiment. This sentiment has induced several different formulations of the nature of "the Quebec problem" and of the strategies most appropriate for English Canada to deal with it. One formulation, which has acquired some support within the "Waffle" group of the New Democratic Party, contends that the aspirations of Quebec nationalism must be met, even though this will probably require a fundamental separation of governmental structures. Other formulations, however, seek to merge Quebec nationalism into a greater pan-Canadian nationalism based upon certain common interests. These interests may lie in a common need to reduce American influence or in class problems that straddle both English and French Canada.

Political Structures: Pluralization of the Party System

The heterogeneity and tension among beliefs is paralleled by a pluralization of party structures. No one party appears able to capture complete possession of power within the Quebec political system. Instead there is an intense struggle among several parties and other political groupings.[26] This pluralization of party structures seems to be rooted in the particular kinds of social change that Quebec has experienced in recent decades.

If we were to regard political groupings as essentially the embodiment of particular political beliefs, then pluralization of structures could be seen as a consequence of the previously discussed impact of

---

Thus, it could be argued that within a significant segment of the population, October support for the War Measures Act was a function of the crisis atmosphere rather than an automatic acceptance of authority – once the crisis atmosphere had dissipated, the right of the government to impose the measure came into question. Significantly, the survey results suggest that this questioning was more widespread in urban areas than in rural areas. Also, it was more widespread among French-Canadian residents of Quebec than English-Canadian residents. Alternatively, one could argue that the November survey misrepresented the intensity of support for the government measures against the FLQ. In November, respondents were forced to register either a simple approval or a simple disapproval – they were not given the opportunity to register a "partial approval."

[26] This pluralization of party support is documented in Vincent Lemieux *et al*, *Une Election de réalignement: l'élection générale du 29 avril 1970 au Québec* (Montreal: Editions du Jour, 1970).

social change upon belief systems. Social change which has induced the formulation of new belief systems, as well as creating new élites to champion them, has in turn necessitated the formation of new party structures to express these new beliefs. For instance, new beliefs about the role of government within French-Canadian society have given rise to the Parti Québécois. FRAP was formed to give recognition of the claim that French Canada is an essentially working-class society. In addition one can cite new parties that were formed to give a clearer expression to old beliefs. It could be argued that parties such as le Ralliement National, and even le Ralliement Créditiste arose, in part at least, because old beliefs about the role of the Church and the nature of authority were not receiving clear expression in the existing party systems.

The extent to which the party system reflects the range of political beliefs in contemporary Quebec can perhaps be more fully appreciated through a systematic classification along the lines of the three central components of belief systems: the nature of French-Canadian society; the role of government in French-Canadian society; and the nature of authority.

At the federal level, all three parties with major support in Quebec – the Liberal Party, the Progressive Conservative Party, and the Ralliement Créditiste – support the belief that French Canada can still benefit from sharing governmental structures with English Canada. The Liberal Party has been especially insistent on encouraging greater French-Canadian participation in the common structures. The Ralliement Créditiste, however, distinguishes itself from the other parties in that it has tended to adhere to more traditional values and structures (thus, it was opposed to any laws on sex and divorce which might contradict the Church's position). Also, it has championed a more traditional approach to authority (maintenance of civil liberties seems to have been given low priority in the struggle against terrorism in October, 1970).

At the provincial level, the ideological differentiation among the parties is highly pronounced. The traditional vision of French-Canadian society, stressing the role of the Church and the virtues of rural life, has been favoured by the Union Nationale throughout the last three decades. This same orientation was pursued during the last election by the new provincial wing of the Ralliement Créditiste. On the other hand, since 1960 the Liberal Party has sought to accelerate the transformation of French Canada to a technological society. This vision was popularized in the early 1960's by the regime of former Premier Jean Lesage, and is receiving renewed expression in the

Bourassa regime's quest for efficiency. The Parti Québécois has similarly embraced the technological society but has sought to combine this with a drive for social and economic equality.

There are wide differences among the parties concerning the role of government in French-Canadian society. The Union Nationale has not sought to expand radically the functions of government. It has become increasingly ambivalent about the advisability of sharing governmental structures with English Canada. On the other hand, the provincial wing of the Ralliement Créditiste, while seeming to share the Union Nationale's reticence to broaden the functions of government, has committed itself to the maintenance of the present federal system. For its part, the Liberal Party has sought to radically expand the functions of government while continuing to support the federal system. Finally, the Parti Québécois has combined an insistence on expanding the functions of government with a firm determination that all the governmental structures should be exclusively Québécois. It contends that this is necessitated by, among other things, the lack of French-Canadian economic power. With respect to the nature of authority, the Union Nationale and the Ralliement Créditiste seem to be less attached to liberal democratic values than the Liberal Party and the Parti Québécois. Thus, in each of the three central components of the French-Canadian belief systems, alternative formulations are represented within the Quebec party system.

In this context, it should be observed that, increasingly, new political groups have arisen outside the established party system. Most of these are concerned with special issues and do not seek to replace existing parties. Examples of such groups would be the Ligue Pour L'intégration Scolaire, Opération McGill, and the Mouvement de Libération du Taxi. A notable exception to this pattern is the Front de Libération du Québec (FLQ). A movement which adheres to the Marx-Marcuse critique of the technological society, the FLQ seeks to transform French Canada into a society where men will be truly "liberated" from all forms of repression. Its vision of French-Canadian society is very different from that represented by the established parties, including the Parti Québécois. Moreover, seeing no prospect of implementing its vision through liberal democratic structures, it asserts the necessity of violence as an instrument to attain its ends, and has already demonstrated a readiness to use violence in an extremely cold-blooded manner. The challenge that the FLQ poses to Quebec seems to lie less in its vision of a totally "liberated" society –

which seems to have little true support – than in its popularization of the doctrine that any kind of social and political change can be effected only through violence. (This may now be somewhat less of a threat on account of the denunciation of violence by Pierre Vallières, the FLQ's one-time philosopher, who, in a message in late 1971, claimed that violence simply strengthened "the power structure's" support in Quebec society.)

Yet this doctrine of violence may continue to appear attractive, particularly to those who feel frustrated in their attempts to obtain change through the existing democratic structures. The sense of frustration may well be intensified by such factors as the rejection by the Trudeau government of Quebec's plan for social policy and constitutional change; the failure of the Parti Québécois to receive legislative representation proportional to its popular support; and the suspension of civil liberties in Quebec until April, 1971.

The foregoing attempt to link the fragmentation of the party system to the pluralization of belief systems may be less satisfying when it is used to explain mass support for these parties, as opposed to support among the more politically active segments of the population. We may find that at the mass level, ideological distinctions between parties are only poorly perceived or are attached little importance (this may even be so with respect to positions on constitutional issues).[27] Nevertheless, in another sense, the particular conditions of social change in Quebec may still be responsible for the inability of any political party to obtain the support of the majority of the electorate. As we have seen, in contemporary Quebec, most elements of French-Canadian society are experiencing severe economic and social dissatisfaction – a dissatisfaction intensified by increased expectations. The precise nature of this dissatisfaction may vary among classes. In the case of the bureaucratic middle class, it results from the necessity of working in English or from the realization that advancement is blocked by Anglophones. In the case of the urban working class, dissatisfaction results from such conditions as low salaries and widespread unemployment. Among the rural population it is similarly a case of low and declining income and of widespread unemployment, but there may also be present a concern over the challenge to traditional values and structures.

[27] This possibility has been developed in the writings of Maurice Pinard. See, for instance, Maurice Pinard, "La rationalité de l'électorat: le cas de 1962," Vincent Lemieux ed., *Quatre élections provinciales au Québec* (Québec: Les Presses de l'Université Laval, 1969), pp. 179-195.

Yet, whatever the sources, we can postulate that over the society as a whole there is a high degree of strain and dissatisfaction. Under these conditions, support for a particular political party will be only conditional. It will be closely tied to the popular evaluation of the performance a party gives when it acquires some degree of control over the governmental apparatus. As long as the conditions of strain remain, we can expect that among French Canadians in Quebec the bases of support for parties will be highly unstable. No one party will be able to retain for long the support of a majority of the voters.[28] There will be a widespread disposition to shift to new and untried political parties. In this way, the particular conditions of social change in Quebec could be responsible for the continued existence of a highly fragmented party system.

CENTRAL POLITICAL CHALLENGES IN THE 1970's

As one traces how profound changes in French-Canadian society have been reflected in the functioning of the Quebec political system, through both a new heterogeneity in political belief systems and a fragmentation of the party system, there emerges a portrait of a society as an independent force with a political system the passive recipient of that society's influences. In the case of Quebec, such an image is, in fact, a fairly accurate characterization of the state of affairs over the last decade. Governments seem to have occupied themselves primarily with seeking to comprehend social change and accommodate it, rather than attempting to master and direct the development of French-Canadian society. Only in the instance of educational reform and, perhaps, the nationalization of the hydro-electric facilities has a Quebec government reversed the pattern and induced profound social change. If French Canada is to continue to exist, it is clear that the Quebec government is going to have to exercise a much greater independent influence on the society. It will have to succeed in reorganizing French-Canadian society in some fundamental ways.

First, if French Canada is going to retain its population, the Quebec government will have to take measures to further the process of trans-

[28] Thus, the May, 1971, survey cited in Note 26 reveals that almost a third of the respondents (31.6 per cent) did not know which party they would support if an election were to be called. Of those who had voted Liberal in the 1970 election, only 57.8 per cent would be ready to vote Liberal again; only 23.4 per cent of those who had voted Union Nationale would again support that party; and only 54.9 per cent of those who had voted Créditiste said they would be prepared to vote Créditiste. The Parti Québecois was the most successful in preserving its clientele (74.5 per cent). (Bellavence and Gilbert, *Le Devoir*).

formation of French Canada into a complete technological society. In particular, French-Canadian cadres will have to assume much greater control of the Quebec economy. (This problem is further aggravated by the fact that the Quebec universities are already preparing candidates for these positions.) In view of the Anglo-Saxon domination of the private sector, this may well require a massive expansion of the public sector. Also, the large, low-income segment of French-Canadian society will have to acquire a more satisfactory share of the benefits of the technological society. This involves steady employment and a drastic improvement in living conditions.

Secondly, if French Canada is to retain its identity, this technological society must be compatible with a full and viable Francophone culture. The essential condition here is that French Canadians should be able to live almost entirely in the French language. In particular, they must be able to work in that language. With the increased integration of the Quebec economy into a continental economy, this goal represents a very difficult challenge. It is not yet clear whether, given even the best of conditions, this challenge can be met. Certainly, it would require major, decisive action on the part of the Quebec government. So far, this has not been in evidence.

Chapter 4

National Economic Patterns: Unemployment, Industrial Diversification, and External Policy

Any understanding of Canada's external policy in the 1970's must include an understanding of the nature of those problems which concern economic development in Canada in this decade, especially those which are more federal than provincial in terms of the public's expectation of leadership. The balance, size, and terms of Canada's foreign trade are the most obviously perceived federal responsibilities. These however cannot be adequately assessed without first assessing other national imperatives such as the need for a national industrial strategy. The necessity for an industrial strategy for Canada as a whole will be discussed here because the problems involved in meeting this are vital to understanding the nature of Canada's pursuit of the first priority of its external policy, that of "economic growth."

Canada's fitful efforts in the late sixties and early seventies to put together a more efficient yet labour-intensive industrial strategy have not been noted for their success. In addition some of the rigidities and costs of foreign ownership are becoming more apparent; it is also clear that the vast expenditure in human capital through secondary, post-secondary education, and training centres has not always been adequately linked to the nature of the employment demand profile in Canada; and the development emphasis on resource industries appears to resemble a policy better suited for producing a surplus on current account in international trade than a policy which meets the long-term employment problem. Let us examine these problems beginning with the latter first.

MANPOWER PATTERNS AND THE EMPHASIS ON RESOURCE
DEVELOPMENT

It is clear from the brief review of provincial economic profiles in
Chapter 2, that all the provincial economies depend to some extent
on resource industries. Canadian exports are heavily concentrated in
such primary materials as wheat, iron, and other metal ores, petroleum, natural gas, wood pulp, newsprint, lumber, flour, aluminum,
coal, primary iron and steel products. Whereas in most industrialized
western countries end-products account for over half of their exports,
end-products (apart from automobiles) account for less than one-fifth
of Canadian exports. Although total Canadian exports of manufactured goods increased in recent years, this rise was due in large measure to the implementation of the U.S.-Canadian Defence Production
Sharing Agreement of 1959 which has yielded a $508 million surplus
since its inception to the end of 1970 (*Financial Post*, October 30,
1971, p. 2); and to the U.S.-Canadian automobile agreements of
1965 which U.S. (but not Canadian) sources estimate to have been
at least one billion dollars in Canada's favour since its inception
(*Financial Post*, October 30, 1971, p. 6). In fact the thinking behind
the economic "game plan" of President Nixon, announced August 15,
1971, by emphasizing more U.S. production and export of manufactured goods clearly implies that the growth of Canada's exports of
such goods to the U.S. could decrease in the early seventies unless the
U.S. economy greatly expands. Also both the Defence Production
Sharing Agreement and the Auto Pact are in the process of being
reversed so as to be more favourable to the U.S. Therefore although
some Canadian analysts had been tentatively optimistic about trends
in Canadian exports of manufactured goods in the late sixties, there
are few optimists now.

Yet what about the other key sector, the primary industries? Here
we see that even though provincial development programs in the past
have depended on primary industry, Canadian manpower needs are
dramatically decreasing in the primary industries as a proportion of
total employment needs to 1975. A 1969 study by the Federal Department of Manpower and Immigration on manpower requirements
reflects changes in manpower patterns which have already taken
place, and it projects to 1975 some of the needs of the economy with
respect to the labour force. The significant pattern which emerges in
this study is that the labour force will become increasingly diversified

in almost all areas of the country, bringing some regions into an employment profile increasingly similar to that of central Canada. The study states that "it is expected that there will be a decline in employment in the primary industries in all regions, though employment in mining and in some regions, forestry, show increases because of the expected effects of new developments and discoveries."[1] Regardless of development plans by provinces, the study projects that regional average rates of employment by industry will slow down in primary industry almost everywhere. In the Atlantic region, agriculture, forestry, fishing, trapping, and mining employment rates are expected to decelerate; in Quebec and B.C., agriculture and forestry; and in the prairie provinces, agriculture is expected to shrink as a source for employment. The decline is traced primarily to the increased mechanization of much of the work in resource industries. These patterns may result in unprecedented new influences on Canadian external policy because they will alter somewhat the nature of pre-1970 provincial pressures. The pattern in the past for almost indiscriminate development of the resource industries – a pattern for which most provinces must bear responsibility as well as the federal government – is being examined more closely in almost all provincial capitals. No longer can it be assumed that Ottawa will be pressured by the provinces outside of central Canada to evolve an industrial strategy that gives little emphasis to employment-generating industries in the non-primary sectors. If a way can be found to locate more such industries outside of central Canada it is clear that a symmetry of concern may emerge between provincial and federal priorities for an industrial strategy.

Projections of employment requirements in various occupations for 1975 make it clear that future needs will be for craftsmen, professional, and technical manpower in all provinces, with a dramatic increase in needs for clerical manpower for Ontario. The Department study projects that "management" (as a category) will maintain its 1961 (8 to 10 per cent) share of total labour force employment to 1975. Professional and technical fields will increase their share from 10 per cent in 1961, to about 15 or 16 per cent by 1975. Clerical, service, and recreation occupations will increase their share slightly in the seventies while sales, transport, commerce, craftsmen, and production process workers will maintain their present shares. The decline in employment share expected in the primary sector is dramatic: from 28 per cent

[1] The data and trends noted in this and the following two paragraphs are found in B. Ahamad, *A Projection of Manpower Requirements By Occupation in 1975* (Ottawa: Department of Manpower and Immigration, 1969), pp. 1-25, 39-60.

(1961), to about 11 per cent by 1975. Labourers (as an employment class) will also have lost some of their share in all regions by 1975 as well. According to this report the greatest inflow into the work force has come and will come in the craftsman, production processing, and related fields. Professional and technical occupations are expected to account for the next highest inflows; service, recreation, and clerical occupations next. All primary occupations except miners, quarrymen, and related workers will continue to face a lack of demand.

These projections however are about the share of the employment pie. But how big will the pie be compared to the total employable work force? Trends on "share of employment" say nothing about how great overall employment will be. It is well-known that Canada has one of the most serious unemployment problems of any major developed country, with unemployment climbing from 359,000 in January, 1966, to over 680,000 in March, 1971. There are fears, in high places, about Canada's expected overall employment performance in the early 1970's. Prime Minister Trudeau has expressed concern about the number of jobs available for young people, and Trade Minister Jean Luc Pepin has admitted to being perplexed about the intractability of the high unemployment rate in Canada.

It seems clear that even if Canadian wheat sales, oil discoveries, and expanding mining and forestry operations help to increase Canada's share of world markets, or meet some of the provincial development hopes, the blunt truth remains: that these "basic activities" of Canada are not labour intensive. In fact, the introduction of many technological and mechanical improvements into these fields has helped to decrease dependence on manpower. The labour productivity of primary industries is climbing faster than for any other work sphere. When put in the context of Canada's international commerce these manpower patterns clash dramatically with trade trends.

Canada will always find it difficult, therefore, to jettison many struggling labour-intensive industries in the non-primary sector for the sake of large foreign orders for primary industries. The continental strategy behind the exemptions granted to Canadian raw materials, but not to many processed exports, by President Nixon on August 15, 1971, was clearly at variance with Canada's employment needs. In fact, one of Prime Minister Trudeau's ministers, Eric Kierans, resigned early in 1971 because he believed the Government was sacrificing, in its tax development and foreign exchange policies, labour-intensive industry for primary capital-intensive activity such as mining. The Canadian trade stance can be made to look unusually protectionist both to foreign capitals *and* to its own western provinces (such as British Columbia, Alberta, and Saskatchewan) if trade figures alone are at issue. Yet employment patterns of the labour force argue a strong case for more diversification of industry in order to open up more labour-intensive activity throughout Canada.

Relevant to this problem of diversification is the Science Council of Canada's rather bleak report released in October, 1971, entitled *Innovation In A Cold Climate: The Dilemma of Canadian Manufacturing*. It points to the serious downward trend in one key, labour-intensive sector of the economy:

> Between 1961 and 1967 manufacturing employment increased almost 25 per cent. In 1968 this growth began to falter and employment has now remained essentially static for the last two years. This development can be traced to a levelling off (and in most cases a decline) in employment in precisely those industries that contributed most heavily to new employment in the first half of the '60's.

Nor does the Council have much hope for a reversal of this trend. It is blunt about the severity of the consequences:

> Canada's economy in this decade will increasingly become dependent on the resource and service industries. Resource industries offer limited opportunities for employment; furthermore, much of their profit does not remain in Canada. This funnelling of funds out of the country is likely to stunt the growth of our service industries.
> Our participation in international trade will become less and less significant and we will become – once again – mainly suppliers of raw materials to the North American continent.

Evidence of this trend may also be seen in the forecasts of expenditures of U.S. corporations in their Canadian affiliates for 1971 and 1972. These forecasts signify a trend away from investment in manufacturing enterprises in Canada toward investment in the extractive industries. A survey of spending plans on plant and equipment taken by the U.S. Commerce Department in June, 1971, before President Nixon announced his new economic program makes the Nixon program appear almost as if it was little more than a confirmation of a trend already underway (see *Globe and Mail*, October 6, 1971, p. B.1). Compared with total 1970 spending of $1,159,000,000 in the manufacturing sector, the 1971 forecast was $1,110,000,000, and the

1972 forecast $1,061,000,000. Within this sector, the U.S.-owned chemical industry in Canada expected a 22 per cent decrease in 1971 and a further 9 per cent drop in 1972. Transportation equipment forecasts for 1971 and 1972 were $173 million and $183 million, compared to $289 million in 1970. In contrast total spending in the non-manufacturing sector – including petroleum and mining and smelting – was $726 million in 1970, and projected to be $796 million in 1971, and $884 million in 1972.

All these developments raise a key consideration vital to any federal government. This consideration links employment to the structure of Canada's trade in the 1970's, and must take into account the continual deterioration of Canada's term of trade if it does not increase exports of products that are manufactured and processed. There is no reason to suspect that the steadily worsening terms of trade for resource industries so obvious in the past two decades will not continue in this decade as well. The past trend is unmistakable. According to the *Canadian Statistical Review*, the price index for crude raw materials exported from Canada was 140.4 in 1968 (the index was 100 in 1948). The prices of end products imported into Canada were indexed at 164.7 in 1968. The worry for Canadians in the 1970's, according to some observers, is that one result of immense investment in developing the resource sector will be that:

> Canadians will be forced to buy more and more U.S. manufactured goods. Over the long haul we will be committing ourselves to purchasing goods whose prices are rising more rapidly than the prices of the goods we sell. We will be forced to sell more and more raw materials to buy back the same quantity of manufactured goods . . . . This dependence of Canadians on raw materials at the expense of manufacturing would mean that we would suffer from a permanent trend towards an increased rate of unemployment.[2]

Yet this cry for "more diversification of industry" and "more manufacturing" in Canada, if frequently exhorted for domestic audiences, is less frequently analyzed in the context of productivity. The problem with many sectors of Canadian industry, apart from the primary sector, is unimpressive productivity compared to the annual increase in labour productivity in primary industries. For example the increase has

[2] James Laxer, in *Canadian Dimension*, April, 1971, p. 15.

been running at 5.6 per cent per year in agriculture, to only 3.8 per cent in "commercial, non-agriculture, goods-producing industries," and only 1.1 per cent per year respectively in commercial service-producing industries from 1946 to 1966.[3]

AN EMERGING INDUSTRIAL STRATEGY?

A tempting but incomplete recommendation for the federal government to follow in the light of the low productivity in the manufacturing sector would be that Canada should cut tariffs to emphasize those industries in the manufacturing and processing sectors which are usually competitive internationally. To some extent the federal department of Industry, Trade, and Commerce took this course in attempting to rationalize the chemical industry. This is frequently described as the Swedish approach to the problem. But in fact, as Sweden has recognized in its own plans, something more than immediate international competitiveness is needed if employment opportunities are to grow in the non-primary sector. Considerations involving the need for research, employment, and income generation will have to supplement the present federal Department of Industry, Trade, and Commerce's stated criterion of international competitiveness. For example, the federal government policy of forcing Canadian chemical companies to cut costs simply forced these companies to shift toward more reliance on their parents for such services as research, planning, development, employee training, and engineering.

To promote a strategy which does not force industries to rationalize, Canadian trade policy-makers will obviously have to take action in three particular directions: firstly, strengthen Canada's weak science and technology base; secondly, institute a clear and vigorous domestic industrial policy; which thirdly, will affect decisions relating to the high degree of foreign ownership in major exporting and technology-based industries. Historically, Canada has relied in the private sector on the research and development of others (see Table 4). For example, in 1965 Canada spent 1.3 per cent of its GNP on research and development compared to 3.4 per cent in the U.S. (see, *Science Forum*, August, 1969, p. 22). From 1964 to 1970 the low indigenous control of the research and development output in Canada is vividly displayed by the fact that of all patents issued in those years "66 per cent were granted to U.S. residents, 29 per cent to residents of other coun-

[3] Ahamad, *op. cit.*, p.45.

tries and only 5 per cent to Canadian citizens,"[4] Research and development expenditures by private industry in Canada actually declined from $340 million in 1969, to $338 million in 1970 (*Financial Post*, June 5, 1971, p. 10).

Table 4. Distribution of National Research and Development Expenditures by Sectors of Performance and Country, 1967

(Percentages)

	Business Enterprise	Government	Higher Education	Private Non-Profit
Switzerland	76.5	6.3	17.1	—
Sweden	69.9	14.2	15.5	0.4
U.S.A.	69.8	14.5	12.2	3.6
Germany	68.2	5.1	16.3	10.4
Belgium	66.8	10.4	21.4	1.3
U.K.	64.9	24.8	7.8	2.5
Japan	62.5	13.0	22.9	1.6
Netherlands	58.1	2.7	17.7	21.5
France	54.2	32.1	12.9	0.8
Canada	37.7	35.6	26.7	

Note: Figures may not add to 100.0% because of rounding.
Source: OECD Document DAS/SPR/70.48, Table IV.

An intensive effort, therefore, may be necessary to improve Canada's research and development performance in certain sectors of the economy. There is some evidence of resolve in federal government policy. More research and development funding is to go into industry as opposed to government laboratories, and a Ministry of Science and Technology has been established to oversee this shift. But officials concede that it will take some years to see the benefits of any such improvement especially since the touchstone of the new science policy, following the ideas of the second volume of the Senate Science Report, is to remove the control of a scientific strategy from the

[4] For these and other figures on Canada's performance in research and development see the Canadian Senate's Report, *A Science Policy For Canada*, Vol. 1 (Ottawa: 1970). For the patent information see p. 136 of this Report.

scientists and to place it with the public and private arms and agencies who are familiar with science. This blending of communication with, and control over, public and private scientists will take some time to become effective and the question still remains whether the new ministry will avoid the two most obvious pitfalls: total captivity by scientists, or vainglorious and insensitive initiatives from government.

Yet a mistake, which might have even more important consequences, would be excessive public funding of research by both foreign and domestic owned firms, which are already heavily protected by the tariff, without first identifying whether it is more efficient in some industrial sectors to encourage firms to purchase research results and technology from abroad through joint ventures, licensing, etc. This may open the way for some Canadian firms to produce at a lower cost, and move into export markets rather than simply subsidize research of over-protected industries.

To date, the Canadian approach to all these problems has been characterized by an *ad hoc*, unplanned diversity, which reflects not only the nature of Canada's industries, but also the methods of attack which have yielded little that is positive or coherent.

For example, efforts to rationalize Canada's chemical industry, which have been underway for several years now, are hampered by the fact that the industry is largely owned or controlled by foreign multinational corporations. Thus, there is no easy rationalization route through mergers and amalgamations since each international corporation is anxious to maintain its separate identity in the Canadian market. The federal government has rejected any solution that would be achieved by a new element of trade protection for the industry, in spite of strong industry pressure. It has not rejected as yet, however, the industry's request for research assistance. In the tire industry, which is entirely foreign-owned, the federal government is proposing that tire manufacturers be allowed to import all specialty tires, currently manufactured duty-free in Canada, so that the companies can concentrate on a much narrower range of items. There is some concern, though, that their U.S. parents will fight such a development.

Within the computer-communications industry, a number of steps are underway to increase Canadian activity and to ensure Canadian ownership in some areas. There are no purely Canadian computer manufacturers, the manufacturing market is currently dominated by

IBM and Digital Equipment Co. of Canada. Other companies, notably Control Data, but also Honeywell, National Cash Register, and Univac, are stepping up their manufacturing efforts in Canada. The Canadian government has taken the position that since Canada is an important market for computer companies – there were 3,548 computers installed in Canada by May 1, 1971 (*Globe and Mail*, November 6, 1971, p. B1) – the major companies have a responsibility to carry out some manufacturing and research and development activity in Canada. All these activities are intended to be designed for international markets and thus are highly specialized. IBM has set up extensive research and development, and manufacturing in Canada, and is building a new assembly plant in Canada, and Control Data is building both a research and development centre and a new manufacturing plant in this country. At the same time, the federal government, through the recently-established Department of Communications, is currently devising policy guidelines for the future computer-communications industry in Canada. A large role is expected to be assigned to the common carriers, which are already largely Canadian-owned, while other measures will be introduced. These will probably include direct research and development assistance, to foster the growth of Canadian-owned computer service and time-sharing organizations so that a large element of the software side of the industry develops under Canadian ownership. Apart from the development of some types of terminal equipment and computer-communication interface devices, Canada will continue to rely on foreign computer technology in hardware. One very important reason for this is the cost of technology development. Canada had hoped to develop its own communications satellites but after a heated domestic debate in 1970 decided that the costs and delivery scheduling of a U.S. corporation, Hughes Aircraft, were more attractive than the costs and timing of Canadian satellite development.

Canada's participation in the aircraft industry is also limited, and largely foreign-owned. A number of major U.S. corporations have plants in Canada, as does one major British corporation. In large measure the industry developed in Canada in the defence sector, with companies building Canadian plants as a condition of military sales to the Canadian Armed Forces. In the mid-50's Canada developed a highly sophisticated military jet of its own, the Avro Arrow, but no other country would buy it, and the project was scrapped at great cost. Since then Canada has worked cautiously to ensure that there is a tolerable level of Canadian manufacturing participation in relation to the country's purchases of military and civilian aircraft. Separately, efforts have been made to develop Canadian expertise in light aircraft, with some success. But sales are never easy. Even the Canadair CL-215 water bomber, tailor-made for forest fire-fighting, is having difficulties finding a buyer from Canada's provincial and federal governments because of departmental disputes over whose departmental budget should pay for it. If that sale is complicated, the experience of the STOL (short take-off and landing aircraft) is far more so. For two years the federal government has examined proposals from the industry in Canada for supportive development costs of a STOL aircraft. A major North American market is expected to develop, but the government is uncertain about the willingness of U.S. airlines to buy from Canada as well as the degree of opposition that may arise in the future over the location of airports within metropolitan centres. The federal government has therefore considered a merger of de Haviland Aircraft of Canada, Ltd. and Canadair Ltd. into a single company. Speculation is that such a merger would require the federal government to buy out, in part, the foreign owners and the newly merged corporation would be jointly owned by the government and foreign shareholders. Two leading foreign aerospace corporations would probably be invited to take minority positions in the new corporation.

The Canadian textile industry is an example of a possibly successful solution, this time using public guidelines. A federal government program, introduced in 1970, will provide financial assistance and temporary tariff protection for sectors of the industry that demonstrate to the satisfaction of a government-industry board that they have serious rationalization plans to participate in domestic and export markets. (Canadian exports of clothing and accessories by 1972 had tripled since 1968).

Yet when all is said and done it has remained easier for Canada to depend on the steady growth of primary industries, and this may have weakened the federal government's will to create and develop a strategy for industrial growth outside the resource industries. Over the next few years the most promising areas of Canadian economic growth remain mineral extraction and processing, energy development, and pipelines. In 1970 about $1.4 billion of copper, nickel, lead, zinc, iron, and other metals, ores, and concentrates were exported. Oil and gas exports to the United States have increased at a rapid rate, and coal exports especially to Japan are rising sharply. Vast development expenditures in the mining, oil and gas industries are expected over the next five years, (see *Globe and Mail*, October 6, 1971, p. 131). At the same time several billion dollars may be poured into the building of new pipelines to carry Canadian, and possibly Alaskan, oil to the central U.S. Yet even the federal government is recognizing that these strong elements of the Canadian economy need to be redirected to provide for emerging new, non-economic priorities. Therefore the government hopes to be able to require mining companies to do more of their processing or refining in Canada.

In addition the Deputy Energy Minister, has warned of further guidelines that would link resource development, environmental protection, increased domestic ownership, and a more diversified industrial strategy for Canada. Such guidelines would ensure that Canadians had enough of their own minerals at a price to stimulate development of secondary industry, even if this meant one price at home and another abroad. The guidelines would also set standards for domestic and foreign-owned companies with respect to pricing, marketing, land tenure, operating practices, processing, degree of foreign ownership and control, employment practices, land conservation, and tenure, reclamation, and integration of land or resource development.[5]

FOREIGN OWNERSHIP AND PROBLEMS OF DIVERSIFIED ECONOMIC
DEVELOPMENT

Although all of the effects of foreign ownership on a development strategy cannot be discussed here, it must be recognized that in devising programs on economic development Canada must contend with two factors unique among industrialized countries – non-residential control of key parts of its economy, and the concentration of that power. The 1968 figures in the Report of the Minister of Industry, Trade and Commerce under the Corporations and Labour Returns Act (December 1970) included the following:[6]

Non-resident ownership of the Canadian economy is largely concentrated in a small number of very large corporations. In 1968 there were 276 foreign-owned corporations in non-financial industries with assets of $25 million or more, representing some 6 per cent of all foreign-owned corporations in the non-financial indus-

[5] See his speech to the Toronto Branch of the Canadian Institute of Mining and Metallurgy, March 25, 1971.
[6] *Annual Report of the Minister of Industry, Trade and Commerce under the Corporations and Labour Returns Act* (Ottawa: December 1970), p.29.

tries reporting to CALURA. These 276 corporations had contained assets of $27.7 billion or 70 per cent of the assets of all non-resident-owned corporations and 28 per cent of all assets of all non-financial corporations, both reporting and non-reporting. This reflected a greater degree of concentration in terms of both numbers and assets than was demonstrated by resident owned corporations. (The 186 Canadian-owned corporations of this asset size represented less than 1 per cent of all reporting Canadian-owned corporations and had assets of $18.0 billion or 43 per cent of their assets.)

The precise amount of concentration and foreign ownership can be seen in Table 5.

Canadian concern about foreign ownership reflects a concern about the economic power of large multinational corporations. Many critics argue that there is a tendency to produce Canadian subsidiaries which are "truncated" because they are mere distributing depots, or mere assembly operations, or mere resource extractors. They worry as well that multinational corporations may also discourage their Canadian subsidiaries from exploiting various export markets. Another frequently voiced concern is that in many cases research and development are concentrated in the country of the parent company; and equally important for any Canadian industrial strategy, the industrial structure resulting from the proliferation of wholly-owned subsidiaries neither lends itself to the type of rationalization that occurs through amalgamation of companies, nor fosters the managerial and other skills necessary for diversified industrial growth. None of these fears are clearly confirmed in the unauthorized Gray Report. According to several Canadian economists they may be exaggerated (see A. E. Safarian, for example, in "Some Myths on Foreign Investment in Canada," in the *Journal of Canadian Studies*, August, 1971; and the speech by the chairman of Canadian General Electric before the Canadian Club, Toronto, Nov. 8, 1971). Yet most economists admit that these fears are valid in some situations, some truncation of Canada's industrial sector does result from foreign ownership in some industries. Other economists reply that critics of foreign investment overlook those key sectors of Canada's economy with low foreign-control. Yet how many of these Canadian-owned sectors are pivotal for innovation and for export initiatives in the manufacturing sector? (for example, utilities, railways, construction, services, fishing, trapping – see Table 5).

Apart from the indeterminate effect of the Gray Report's recommendations for screening foreign investment only one major policy measure, the establishment of the Canada Development Corporation, is in place to attack the twin problem of foreign ownership and the development and diversification of Canadian-owned companies. The CDC is a $2 billion investment company, whose initial $250 million of equity will come from the federal government.[7] Ultimately, the government is expected to hold only 10 per cent of the shares with the rest, over a period of years, being sold to the public. Only Canadians may buy common shares although non-residents may acquire non-voting preference shares if the directors of the CDC so choose. The CDC, which is expected to operate independently from government, and with the profit needs of shareholders uppermost in mind, will initially take over several government-owned corporations, including the multinational Polymer Corp., the uranium mining and refining company, Eldorado Nuclear Ltd., and Northern Transportation Co., which provides carrier services in the Canadian north. It will also acquire the government's 45 per cent holding in Panarctic Oils Ltd., an oil and gas exploration company with extensive interests in the Canadian Arctic.[8] But one of CDC's most important roles, in the view of the government, is to improve Canada's industrial structure: by providing equity capital for projects involving new or capital intensive technologies; to help rationalize industries through the formation of new companies and through the encouragement of mergers; and by providing for more Canadian participation in resource development and processing industries. It will, according to the former Finance Minister, concentrate its efforts on promising areas of the economy where there is not otherwise likely to be a sufficient degree of Canadian ownership. The Minister has said, "Business and industry have entered a new period of internationalism which makes it desirable that there be a number of Canadian-controlled corporations with headquarters in Canada and with the kind of institutional strength and management capabilities to compete successfully in Canadian and international markets." CDC, he declared, "should emphasize areas involving the development and application of new technology, those which involve the exploitation and utilization of Canadian natural resources, those which have special relevance to the development of the North, and those in which Canada now has or can

[7] Finance Minister Edgar Benson, February 22, 1971, in the House of Commons.
[8] *Ibid.*, see *Debates*, 1971, p.3630.

Table 5.　Average Asset Size of Foreign-owned and All
Corporations, by Industries, Non-financial Industries Only, 1968

Industries in decreasing order of assets size	*Average assets*		Foreign-owned corporations as per cent of total all corporations[1]	
	All Corpora- tions[1]	Foreign- owned Corporations	*Corporations*	*Assets*
	$'000,000			%
Petroleum & coal products	80.7	197.9	40.7	99.7
Tobacco products	19.2	24.9	65.4	84.5
Metal mining	14.7	31.5	20.7	44.2
Primary metal	14.7	52.4	15.5	55.2
Paper & allied industries	14.3	26.8	20.9	38.9
Public utilities	8.3	14.7	8.9	15.7
Communications	7.4	2.1	1.3	.4
Mineral fuels	6.7	20.5	26.8	82.3
Rubber products	5.7	17.0	31.2	93.1
Transport equipment	5.1	19.9	22.2	87.0
Electrical products	3.3	7.1	29.6	64.0
Chemicals & chemical products	3.0	7.7	32.2	81.4
Beverages	2.8	10.8	4.6	17.8
Textile mills	2.1	9.7	11.2	52.0
Machinery	2.1	6.2	24.9	72.2
Transportation	1.9	7.2	2.2	8.4
Non-metallic mineral products	1.7	10.2	8.5	51.6
Storage	1.4	8.6	4.0	24.7
Food	1.3	6.7	6.8	36.0
Other mining	.9	7.3	6.8	57.1
Wood industries	.9	6.6	4.2	30.8
Knitting mills	.7	2.1	7.0	21.9
Metal fabricating	.7	3.5	9.7	46.7
Leather products	.6	1.8	7.1	22.0
Miscellaneous manufacturing	.5	2.5	11.1	53.9
Furniture industries	.4	2.0	3.8	18.8
Printing, publishing & allied industries	.4	3.3	2.6	21.0

Table 5. Continued

Industries in decreasing order of assets size	Average assets		Foreign-owned corporations as per cent of total all corporations[1]	
	All Corporations[1]	Foreign-owned Corporations	*Corporations*	*Assets*
Wholesale trade	.4	2.4	5.6	31.4
Clothing industries	.3	1.9	2.4	13.2
Construction	.3	5.1	.8	13.8
Agriculture, forestry, fishing & trapping	.2	1.0	1.3	6.4
Retail trade	.2	4.8	1.1	21.2
Services	.2	2.7	1.4	19.7
Non-financial – Total	.8	8.1	3.8	39.4

[1] Includes corporations not reporting under CALURA.
Source: Report of the Minister of Industry, *Trade and Commerce Under the Corporations and Labour Returns Act* (December, 1970), p. 33.

develop significant comparative advantages by international standards."[9]

ECONOMIC DEVELOPMENT THROUGH EDUCATION? PROBLEMS AND PROSPECTS

In the past it may have been alleged that Canada could not supply the human resources for a diversified economy or for an industrial strategy based on a Canadian owned and operated technological or manufacturing sector because of Canada's weak educational base. In the 1970's, however, such an allegation is not defensible. Canada is now expending vast sums on education – over a third of most provincial government budgets.

Canada of course has had considerable catching up to do. It has been estimated that education at all levels accounted for 11.4 per cent of the growth in real national income in Canada from 1929 to 1957. For the U.S., however, estimates are 23 per cent for the same period.

The contribution of education to national income from 1950 to 1962

[9] *Ibid.*, p.3638.

in Canada is estimated to have been 5 per cent while for the U.S. it
has been estimated at 15 per cent.[10] Canadian expenditure *per capita*
on education was the same in money terms in 1945 as it was in 1926,
so it actually fell in real terms.[11]

Considerable reform has since occurred in Canada. In 1950, 2.6
per cent of the GNP was expended on formal education, this increased
to 6.5 per cent of GNP by 1966, and will be close to 10 per cent by
1974. The Chairman of the Economic Council of Canada, in a
speech in Toronto in early 1971, noted that government spending in
universities for operating expenses alone increased at an average of
22 per cent a year in the 1960's (*Toronto Star*, May 11, 1971).
"Enrolment increased 50 per cent faster in Canada than in the United
States and costs per student increased about 70 per cent faster in
Canada."

The impact of this increased education will be varied and hard to
predict. Yet, some, perhaps too-sanguine projections of improvement
in employment rates, might be hazarded, based on past correlations.
Differences in education have correlated with employment levels regionally (although the correlation may be coincidental). From 1960-
64, for example, the ratio of employed to total population varied
from a low of 27 per cent in the Atlantic provinces to a high of 37 per
cent in Ontario. The unemployment rate has been highest in those
regions that have spent relatively less on education. The unemployment rate over the post-war period has averaged 7.6 per cent in the
Atlantic region compared to 3.2 per cent in Ontario. In 1961, 4.7 per
cent of the Ontario labour force had university degrees; the Atlantic
rate ranged from 1.7 per cent in Newfoundland, to 3.7 per cent in
Nova Scotia. In that year, expenditure per child on education varied
from $141 in Newfoundland, to $209 in Nova Scotia, while Ontario
spent $335 per child.[12] If the less depressed regions of Canada contin-
ue to spend more money on education there may be some hope for
lower unemployment rates. Apart from these correlations, some other
projections of manpower placement have been made based primarily
on past trends, and they are less optimistic. For example, as we have
noted, the Department of Manpower and Immigration study of Canada's highly qualified manpower finds that there will be a greater
demand for professional and technical occupations than for manual

[10] Ahamad, *op. cit.*, p.49.
[11] *Ibid.*
[12] *Ibid.*, p. 55.

occupations. Professionals and technicians are expected to account for 15 per cent of the labour force by 1975, an increase from 10 per cent in 1961. The earnings of this group have a significant impact on the economy, accounting for 14 per cent of total earnings, but only 10 per cent of the labour force in 1961.[13] Yet this group is a smaller proportion of the maritime work force than the proportion found in the two richest provinces.[14]

One result seems certain however. The growth of this professional and technical group is likely to affect immigration patterns. The increased pool of educated Canadians for professional and technical jobs will mean that Canada will offer immigrant manpower fewer employment opportunites in these jobs than in the past. In 1961 about one-quarter of Canadian immigrants belonged to the professional and technical category. In some occupations such as architecture, medicine, and university education the number of immigrants exceeded the number of Canadian graduations. Net professional immigration to Canada formed 44 per cent of domestic graduations in 1966.[15] In 1961 there were 280,000 university graduates in the Canadian labour force forming 4.3 per cent of the total work force.[16] Only one-third of the 628,000 people in the professional and technical groups that year were university graduates, although a further 45 per cent had undertaken some university education.[17] Canadian university enrolments have quadrupled since 1957, increasing from 73,000 then to about 300,000 in 1971-72, thus promising to mitigate dependence on immigrant flow.

Varying degrees of enrolment are evident in different disciplines. Pure science and education, as fields, increased by 450 per cent between 1957 and 1967. Arts enrolment almost quadrupled in the same period. A marked lack of growth occurred in that decade in engineering and medicine, with rates of 42 per cent and 7 per cent respectively. The social sciences granted the largest share of master's degrees from 1957 to 1967, while the life and physical sciences accounted for almost 60 per cent of all doctorates awarded in 1967. The least growth was in the biological sciences (life science) where gradua-

[13] A. G. Atkinson *et al., Canada's Highly Qualified Manpower Resources* (Ottawa: Dept. of Manpower and Immigration, 1970) pp. 2, 3, 25.
[14] Ahamad, *op. cit.*, p. 57.
[15] Atkinson, *op. cit.*, p. 24.
[16] *Ibid.*, p.13.
[17] *Ibid.*, pp.15-21.

tions showed a less than 100 per cent increase from 1957 to 1967, while all fields averaged a 170 per cent growth.[18]

The supply of physicians for Canada, however, still depends greatly on immigrant manpower. The Royal Commission on Health Services noted:

> Out of nearly 15,000 newly registered physicians in Canada during the years 1950 to 1960 about one-third were immigrant physicians. Over the same years the immigrant doctors were equal to about one-half of total output of 9,300 graduates of Canadian medical schools.[19]

While the physician-population ratio has improved over the last 30 years in Canada, regional distribution is very uneven, and the distribution of Canadian-born doctors is even worse (61.4 per cent of Newfoundland physicians were foreign-born compared to 14.1 per cent in Quebec;[20] the physician-population ratio in Newfoundland is 1:1,484 compared to Quebec's 1:770).[21]

One way to determine a nation's ability to supply manpower for technological advance in secondary as well as primary industry is to survey its scientists and engineers. Both availability plus some unique utilization of both groups seems clear in Canada. Almost half of those surveyed in the Department of Manpower Study,[22] were employed in the engineering field, 13 per cent in the physical sciences, 11 per cent in life sciences, and 9 per cent in social sciences and, finally, 3 per cent in architecture. Engineering employment was most commonly in the electrical, civil, industrial, and mechanical fields in that order. In the physical sciences most were employed in chemistry; in the life sciences most were employed in agricultural work. Economics and statistics dominated the social sciences.[23] Generally, using 1960's labour participation rates, it appears that scientists and engineers residing in Canada were quite fully utilized, since only 7.4 per cent of the survey group were not in the labour force and most of these were still students. Only a small group – 6 per cent – retired from this highly qualified group before the age of 55. (Almost two-thirds of all scientists and

[18] For the data in this paragraph see *ibid.*, pp. 25-31.
[19] Royal Commission on Health Services, *Medical Manpower In Canada*, Volume 1 (Ottawa: 1964), p. 9.
[20] Atkinson, *op. cit.*, p. 131.
[21] *Ibid.*, p. 139.
[22] *Ibid.*, p. 57.
[23] *Ibid.*, p. 4.

engineers in Canada are in industrial work; 20 per cent are employed by government, and 14 per cent by education.) Half of the architects in Canada are *self-employed*; of the other half, 90 per cent work in industry, and 10 per cent in government. Seventy-nine per cent of engineers are hired by industry. In the physical sciences there is an even split among industry, education, and government; life sciences are divided mainly between industry (41.3 per cent) and government (44.5 per cent). The social sciences are represented 61.2 per cent by industry, 14.5 per cent education, and 23.4 per cent government or education.[24]

Yet in the 1970's unemployment, not inadequate supply, may face Canada in several categories of highly trained manpower. Enrolment in graduate studies has climbed 20 per cent per year since 1965. By 1970, Dr. Frank Kelly of the Science Council of Canada reported that, "it must be concluded that permanent employment is available for only one half of this year's output" (*Financial Post*, September 18, 1971, p. 33). Turning to categories of graduate work most vital for technological and industrial advance it is clear that although unemployment has not been a problem for Canadian scientists and engineers in the past it will become so in the future. (Although the academic year 1971-2 showed a decrease in the growth of enrolment in graduate programs in Canada.)

For example a former deputy minister of manpower, W. R. Dymond, has accused the federal government of failing to recognize the enormity of the problem. "The overwhelming governmental emphasis on [forestalling summer student unemployment] to the almost complete exclusion of the more fundamental problem of unemployment among graduates, means that the problem has either fallen through the cracks of federal provincial jurisdiction, or that the ordering of governmental priorities is seriously distorted."[25] Although the seasonally adjusted unemployment rate dropped to "only" 6 per cent of the labour force in March, in 1971 it was soon on the rise again. In June, 1971, over a million students poured into the labour force looking for summer work, and 350,000 new graduates were seeking permanent jobs. Dymond points out that over the decade of the 1960's, the "combined rate of increase of post-secondary graduations (that is, graduates of universities and community colleges) has been of the order of 448 per cent . . . the only comprehensive data we have on demand [for these graduates] is the increase in the total numbers

[24] For the data in this paragraph see *ibid.*, pp. 60, 61.
[25] *Toronto Star*, May 12, 1971, p. 16; quoted by permission of the *Star*.

employed in technical and professional occupations over the decade. ... Employment of this group has increased from 578,000 in 1960, to 1,038,000 in 1969. This represents a rate of increase of about 200 per cent over the decade." Although Dymond has cautioned that the figures are not exact, he has said "it is highly improbable that any pattern of demand that one can reasonably contemplate, would be likely to conform to the pattern of supply that the combined graduation and immigration represents." In general he concludes that the majority of 1971 graduates were in fields in which the labour market prospects were "not favourable in terms of the numbers graduating." For example, pass-arts graduates were "approximately 15 per cent larger in numbers," according to Dymond, but the job market was even more competitive than it was in 1970 (*Toronto Star*, May 12, 1971, p. 16).

A special survey of the labour force in 1971 showed that among persons aged fourteen to twenty-four, full-time students in March, 1971, who did not plan to return to school 67,000 were unemployed in the reference week September 18, 1971, (House of Commons, *Debates*, 1971, p. 9951).

A background study for the Science Council of Canada, in a survey taken in 1965 found less than 15 per cent of scientists and engineers in Canada were employed in research and development compared to approximately 35 per cent in the U.S., 24 per cent in West Germany, 22 per cent in Sweden, and 19 per cent in the U.K.[26] It also shows Canada's rather weak performance compared to other countries in terms of research and development expenditures as a percentage of GNP. In Canada governments are the main employer of research people while industry is the main employer for development work.[27] These findings may reflect a lack of research opportunities in Canada in the private sector. A recent Senate study proposes therefore a doubling of government spending for research with an increased emphasis on applied research for industry as compared to pure research done in universities. Although no amount of government spending can fully make up for the fact that in several sectors Canada's branch plant economy will leave the country with less research activity since parent companies prefer to do this work else-

---

[26] R. W. Jackson, D. W. Henderson, B. Leung; "Background Studies in Science Policy: Projections of Research and Development Manpower and Expenditures," *Study No. 6, Science Council of Canada* (Ottawa: Queen's Printer 1969).

[27] Atkinson, *op. cit.*, p.81.

where and subsidiaries are uniquely placed to import technological discoveries and applications from their parents, government aid may help significantly, however, in applied research and development, perhaps less significantly in pure research.

Moving from university educated to the other trained and untrained parts of the labour market the outlook, if not one of impending crisis, is not one of optimism either. Figures released by the Department of Manpower and Immigration, September 27, 1971, show that a downward trend is becoming increasingly evident in the ability of the department's manpower centres to place workers who are being trained or simply looking for work through these centres. The shrinking number of job placements is evident in all provinces except for the Maritimes where modest increases in placements have occurred (see Table 6).

Since 1966 the department has spent almost $1.4 billion on occupational training (second only to Sweden among Western countries). The Economic Council of Canada, in its Eighth Annual Review, worried about this spending in terms not dissimilar to the emphasis of this chapter:

> Manpower policy is conceived of in Canada largely as a policy affecting the supply side of the market. In Sweden, however, manpower policy is far more comprehensive in scope in that it controls many expenditure programs affecting the level and location of employment and thus operates on the demand side of the market too.

The Council found in fact that the number of trainees in given occupational groups was not related to departmental forecasts of the needs for workers with those skills. "Nor were trainees concentrated in those occupations that had been growing most rapidly."

CONCLUSION

The purpose of this chapter is to raise questions about three fundamental tenets of Canadian economic development since World War II: the belief that expansion of a trained labour supply through education and training will somehow find a suitable demand pattern; that economic sovereignty is not a key part of job creation; and that an emphasis on Canada's unique economic source of wealth – its natural resources – will give Canada not only a firm foothold in international trade, but ensure adequate job creation as well. Although emphasis

Table 6. Department of Manpower and Immigration Placements through Manpower Centres

Province	Canada Manpower Centres Placements (excluding casuals)					National Employment Service Placements (excluding casuals)	
	1970-1971	1969-1970	1968-1969	1967-1968	1966-1967	1965-1966	1964-1965
Newfoundland	16,164	12,589	10,009	7,806	7,468	9,072	6,219
Prince Edward Island	6,648	6,178	4,876	4,170	5,260	6,062	6,336
Nova Scotia	29,049	28,693	23,888	22,103	22,586	25,675	26,089
New Brunswick	22,979	22,572	18,738	20,274	24,408	32,852	30,864
Quebec	148,836	159,842	156,146	189,924	220,548	274,817	295,411
Ontario	239,837	271,338	289,792	268,744	310,887	336,284	320,811
Manitoba	27,929	34,961	37,008	38,011	38,814	41,509	41,883
Saskatchewan	16,811	20,713	24,435	28,275	28,704	29,052	27,912
Alberta	52,416	66,283	67,894	68,852	73,202	77,505	70,758
Northwest Territories*	1,261	858	–	–	–	–	–
British Columbia	85,572	97,132	91,919	94,562	108,976	128,167	114,900
Yukon**	1,464	1,673	–	–	–	–	–
Canada	648,966	722,832	724,705	742,721	840,853	960,995	941,183

* Northwest Territories reported in Alberta provincial totals for the fiscal years 1968-1969 to 1964-1965.
** Yukon reported in British Columbia provincial totals for the fiscal years 1968-1969 to 1964-1965
Source: *Man 751*, Department of Manpower and Immigration; and House of Commons, *Debates*, 1971, p. 8177.

on all three tenets may have been justified at certain stages in Canada's history, and will not therefore be summarily jettisoned, they will undoubtedly fall under more sustained critical examination than ever before.

Hugh Trevor-Roper, a noted British historian, has suggested that "any society so long as it is, or feels itself to be, a working society tends to invest in itself: a military society tends to become more military, a bureaucratic society more bureaucratic, a commercial society more commercial, as the status and profits of war, or office, or commerce are enhanced by success and institutions are formed to forward it."[28] This caveat may be appropriate to Canada's economic development. Ever since World War II, and before that in the case of the emphasis on resource industries, Canada has tended to reinvest ever more deeply in policies reflected in the three attitudes expressed in the above paragraph. It is clear that many Canadians think it is time to re-consider these policies. Already to an unprecedented degree government studies and independent Councils are engaged in such reappraisals. What is striking about the unauthorized version of the Gray Report on foreign ownership (published by the *Canadian Forum*, December, 1971), the Science Council's October, 1971 report on Canada's manufacturing industry, the Ontario Government's Report on Foreign Ownership (released December 8, 1971), and the Eighth Annual Review of the Economic Council of Canada is not so much their concern about the need for a well-developed industrial strategy for Canada, but their re-examination of what hitherto were almost unquestioned tenets of the orthodox view of economic development in Canada.[29]

Any basic shift in policy on these issues will surely have to come from the federal government because all these problems raise questions which relate directly to federal responsibility and in part to external policy, namely: Canada's balance, terms and structure of foreign trade, as well as the link between foreign trade and foreign ownership. There is nothing novel in this special responsibility to be

[28] Hugh Trevor-Roper, *The Rise of Christian Europe* (London: 1965), p.184.
[29] Perhaps the most outspoken reassessment however came from a Trudeau Cabinet minister Eric Kierans, after his resignation. See his "Contribution of the Tax System to Canada's Unemployment And Ownership Problems," Luncheon Address, Annual Meeting of the Canadian Economic Association, Memorial University, St. John's Newfoundland, June 3-5, 1971; and his comments before the convention of the Committee for An Independent Canada, December 11, 1971, in Thunder Bay, Ontario, as reported by the *Globe and Mail*, December 13, 1971, p. 9.

faced by the federal government. What may be novel about the 1970's however is the growing realization by provincial governments, ordinarily totally suspicious of central Canadian priorities, that their employment profiles are becoming more similar to central Canada, and this may open the way for a more unified and nationally accepta- ble industrial ownership and trade strategy for Canada.

If such a strategy evolves, the impact on Canadian external rela- tions will be obvious and the first priority of Canadian foreign policy to promote Canadian "economic growth" will shift to one which emphasizes more selectively those sectors of the economy which must expand and those which should grow more slowly. Simply to state the priority this way is to raise more questions about the pattern of Canada's economic relations with foreign countries than the White Paper on Foreign Policy ever considered. To this extent therefore the White Paper's view of foreign policy in the 1970's is only partially prophetic. Its emphasis on economic relations is prophetic yet its failure to discuss the necessary patterns of those relations is to miss what may be the most important feature of those relations this dec- ade.

Chapter 5

Canadian Trade and the Search for Markets Beyond the United States

TRADE: THE DECLINE OF THE CANADIAN-AMERICAN STRATEGY OF LIBERALIZATION?

Canada's trade patterns are obviously a major part of any industrial development strategy in the 1970's. Exports are probably more important as a component of economic growth in Canada than in any other major industrial nation. In 1970 over-all exports were equivalent to 20 per cent of the country's $84 billion gross national product – – a greater proportion of GNP than is the case in Japan, a well-known trading nation, for example. Yet Canada is the only major industrial nation in the world without direct participation in a market of 100 million or more people. Although Canada's most important export market is the United States, ($10,641,118,837 exports in 1970, and estimated at $10,987,200,000 of Canada's $17,847,500,000 exports in 1971)[1] which consumed 65 per cent of Canada's total exports, and 84 per cent of Canada's manufactured exports in 1970, Canada's overall access to the U.S. manufactured goods market has never been very impressive. It is likely to remain unimpressive given the protectionist tone of the Americans and Canada's disinclination to move to freer trade with the United States. In fact preliminary figures released early in 1972 showed that crude materials formed 26.6 per cent of Canadian exports in 1971, up from 26.1 per cent in 1970. Fabricated materials declined to 33.7 per cent from 34.4 per cent (*Toronto Star*, February 7, 1972, p. 11).

Although most trade officials in Canada, before the August 15,

[1] *Trade of Canada: Exports by Countries, January-December 1970*, Vol. 24, #4 (65-003) (Ottawa: Dominion Bureau of Statistics), p. 351. The 1971 estimate appears in the *Globe and Mail*, January 14, 1972, p. B1.

1971, Nixon policy announcement, were looking for at least a 5 per cent increase in exports in 1971 from the previous year's level of $16.9 billion, imports were expected even then to increase to about 10 per cent from the 1970 level of $13.8 billion. Preliminary figures released early in 1972 showed Canadian exports increased to $17.8 billion, and imports to $15.6 billion (*Toronto Star*, February 7, 1972, p. 11). These expectations centred on the revival of industrial investment, which would boost machinery and equipment imports, and the continuing high value of the Canadian dollar, making a variety of consumer goods imports more attractive.

The first year of the seventies will no doubt reflect much of the pattern of Canadian trade for the next few years. It is a position that may well become intrinsic should President Nixon's "game plan" for the American economy remain a priority for the decade. Exports of grains, minerals and energy resources accounted for much of the 14 per cent growth in Canadian exports in 1970. Of the $1.955 billion increase in exports, grains accounted for a $341 million increase, and iron ore-nickel-copper-lead for $722 million of the increase.[2] All are expected to be strong growth segments for most of this decade. The world grain outlook has improved for Canada; U.S. requirements for Canadian energy resources are continuing to grow; U.S., European, and Japanese demand for Canadian mineral resources shows little sign of abating.

Exports of manufactured goods, however, showed little increase in 1970, rising by only 4 per cent (the General Motors strike in the final quarter reduced this increase somewhat) to $5.9 billion.[3] As mentioned previously, this sector is of greatest concern to the Canadian government since manufactured goods tend to have the greatest Canadian value-added content and hence the greatest employment potential. Much of the strength in the manufacturing sector in 1970 again came from motor vehicles and parts, which accounted for just over 60 per cent of Canada's total manufactured goods exports. Important here is the Canada-U.S. auto pact which, since implementation in 1965, has led to a massive restructuring of the automotive industry in Canada. The industry is owned by the four major U.S. producers together with the larger U.S. auto parts companies. The binational agreement has vastly increased two-way trade between the

[2] See *ibid.*, especially exports to the U.S., China, Japan and U.K. to explain these increases.
[3] See Note 2, Chapter 2.

two countries. Under the auto pact, there is virtual free trade in new vehicles and parts within the industry in North America. Before U.S. administration pressure to have the pact renegotiated, Canadian trade officials were looking for an increase in automotive exports in the next few years because Canadian plant specialization to the compact-sized car portion of the market coincided with a shift in U.S. consumer demand toward smaller cars. It was expected, however, that auto parts producers would fare less well because the increased value of the Canadian dollar made their exports less attractive in U.S. plants, and imports from the U.S. relatively cheaper in Canadian plants. Since 1965 Canadian automotive exports to the U.S. have increased from $230 million to $4.1 billion by 1971, therefore in 1970, manufactured products accounted for about 37 per cent of total exports, compared to about 18 per cent in 1964. Fabricated materials, including metals, newsprint, chemicals, lumber and pulp, shrank to about 37 per cent in 1970 from about 46 per cent in 1964, while crude materials, such as mineral ores, concentrates, and energy resources, accounted for 26 per cent of exports in 1970, compared to about 37 per cent in 1964.[4] The shift to manufactured exports would, of course, have been much less dramatic if the effects of the auto pact were excluded. (Perhaps the strongest examples of exports in manufactured products, aside from automobiles, were exports of communications equipment, which rose from $35 million in 1964, to $218 million in 1970, and exports in office machines and equipment, including computer components, which rose from $44 million in 1964 to $132 million by 1970.)[5]

Another factor central to almost all calculations concerning Canadian trade in this decade is the value of the Canadian dollar. In May, 1962, the Canadian dollar was pegged at 92.5 U.S. cents, a substantial devaluation from its above-par value in the fifties and start of the sixties. This substantial cut was a major stimulative element in the growth of Canadian exports through the sixties. But on May 31, 1970, the federal government unpegged the dollar in the face of strong speculative pressures. Since then it has floated upward to around par with the U.S. dollar. And although the government is committed to an eventual repegging, it does not want to do this until it floats down to the 95-96 U.S. cents range. This appears to be a highly unlikely development. This jump in the value of the Canadian dollar since June 1970 is creating problems for many secondary man-

---

[4] See these estimates in the *Globe and Mail*, January 5, 1971, p. B1.
[5] *Ibid.*

ufacturers dependent on exports who are already operating on slim profit margins. Some manufacturers have lost important business and a small number of plant shutdowns have resulted, while a number of others may not be able to continue to absorb the impact of the higher dollar trade costs. Some, whose export prices were quoted in U.S. dollars, such as pulp and newsprint producers (whose combined exports were $1.9 billion in 1970), have been able to effect some increase in prices but are still hard-pressed on profits. Yet many manufacturers are not in a position to increase prices and the question for them is how much longer they can continue to absorb the effects of the higher-priced dollar.[6]

Because of these basic trading trends, and the priorities for Canada implicit in the Nixon administration's economic policy, a great deal of concern has swept through Canada, as it appears that an extremely harsh U.S.-Canada environment will be inevitable in the 1970's. This new atmosphere may yield greater demand for Canadian resources, but it will also produce a greater squeeze on Canadian non-primary industry. By the late sixties it appeared that the Canadian government suspected this harsh development to occur, and believed that Canada could not really develop competitive industry of its own unless it has access to broader markets. To ensure this access Canada looked to U.S. leadership for world trade liberalization as a precondition for freer U.S.-Canadian trade, realizing that a gradual elimination of tariffs would also eliminate the need for many foreign companies to locate in Canada and would open existing Canadian industry to much stronger competition. (Canada therefore became concerned with providing a domestic environment for economic creativity and efficiency. Programs of tax reform and industrial competition policy provided some important indications of how the government decided to proceed in this direction. Both intimated that Canadian-owned companies would be encouraged in various ways, and that mergers in industries aiming for greater export performance would be treated more liberally than mergers for other purposes.) Yet now it appears Canada cannot depend on American leadership to promote increased world trade liberalization. The basic underpinning of the Canadian policy has been removed, and a relapse into protectionist blocs is more than a distinct possibility.

For example before the Nixon economic policy was announced on

[6] *Ibid.*

August 15, 1971, Canada's most immediate concern was the entry of Britain into the European Economic Community along with other states seeking associate or special relationship with the Community. Originally it was feared that if Britain adopted the EEC's common external tariff and common agricultural policy, some 64 per cent of Canadian exports, $1.48 billion, would face a tariff of some kind, compared to simply 6 per cent before. Britain requested special arrangements for 12 industrial materials. Some of these were granted and are of interest to Canadian exporters. Newsprint, construction grade plywood, phosphorous, nickel and copper will not be subjected to any tariff at all, but aluminum will face a 7 per cent tariff, and tobacco and barley exports will be effectively shut out of the EEC. In all, it is estimated that 28 per cent of Canada's current exports to the U.K. will be affected by Britain's entry to the common market.[7]

The Canadian government is also concerned about Canada's continuing inability to penetrate the EEC and Japanese markets with exports of manufactured products. Although Canada sold some $1.2 billion of exports to EEC members in 1970, only about 14 per cent consisted of manufactured goods.[8] And while exports to Japan amounted to $793 million in the same year, not quite 3 per cent consisted of manufactured products. Canada's principal exports to the Common Market and Japan consist of mineral resources and foodstuffs, especially grains.[9]

The dominating pattern of Canadian trade however will remain: it is likely that close to two-thirds of Canadian exports will continue to go to the U.S. market in the years ahead. As this pattern persists, it will be accompanied, as usual, by continual Canadian expressions of hope that emphasis on U.S. markets can be reduced.[10] Ever since the

---

[7] For a discussion of Canadian-British Trade see *Financial Post*, October 30, 1971.

[8] See exports classified as manufactured for the six EEC countries in reference in Note 1.

[9] *Ibid.*, p. 185.

[10] See for example the argument of Mitchell Sharp, Canada's External Affairs Minister, in a speech in Toronto on November 6, 1971. "In our economic policies we should strive to avoid unnecessary dependence upon the United States, by promoting trade and financial links with the rest of the world. Yet . . . we are not going to strengthen our economy by anti-American policies. . . .

It is our destiny and good fortune to share the North American continent with the richest nation on the earth's surface. It makes good sense to exploit that advantage for all it is worth. It makes good sense to work with the United States for our mutual benefit."

turn of the century these expressions of hope have been irrepressible (usually articulated more by the Conservative party than by the Liberals). The most comprehensive example of this is the Canadian White Paper on Foreign Policy in 1970 which claims to have identified some encouraging new dimensions for Canadian external (mostly trade) policy. A brief examination of these new dimensions might help in a realistic assessment of how Canada's industrial strategy and provincial development programs may be enhanced within a global context. Although Canada's trade with China and the Soviet Union has increased during the last decade (China is now Canada's sixth biggest customer, and the Soviet Union ran a $92 million deficit with Canada in 1970) no official Canadian Government statement has projected a vast increase in exports to these two nations even after the establishment of diplomatic relations with Peking, or after Premier Kosygin's Canadian tour in October, 1971. The emphasis of the Foreign Policy White Paper centred explicitly on three geographical aggregations, the Pacific, Western Europe, and Latin America. As part of the government's piece-meal, *ad hoc* search for less reliance on U.S. trade, let us look at the substance behind these hopes.

THE PACIFIC: CANADA'S "NEW WEST"

Prime Minister Pierre Elliott Trudeau has changed the definition of Canada's relations with the Pacific area by referring to the constellation of nations there, as "a new west" for Canada, a possible focus and opportunity for Canadian external policy, rivalling Canada's past attachment to Europe. His Government's White Paper on Foreign Policy states:

> The Pacific is both Canada's third largest market (after the U.S. and Western Europe) and Canada's third largest supplier. It is an area in which Canada has been an important net direct investor. . . . [Also] the Pacific provides Canada with a surplus of foreign earnings with which to meet trade and payment deficits with the rest of the world.

The GNP of the Pacific non-communist countries has doubled in

---

Mr. Sharp argued further that pursuing relations with other countries – avoiding overdependence on the United States – is "not anti-American in any sense. It is traditional Canadian policy, which is becoming more and more relevant as Europe and Japan, for example, challenge the predominant position of the United States as an economic power and the Soviet Union looks outward for trade with the non-Communist world."

the last ten years and is expected to redouble by 1980. During the 1958-68 period, Canadian exports to Pacific countries increased 416.8 per cent as against 175 per cent to the world, while imports from the Pacific rose 306 per cent compared to 138 per cent from the world. Canadian exports to the countries of the Pacific in 1968 amounted to almost $1,098 million, and imports to some $640 million.[11] Enthusiasm about all this is growing on Canada's West Coast and in the Prairies, and it promises to affect central Canada too, if the search for counterweights to American influence in Canada's international trade is serious. The Australian and South Korean economies are steadily improving and Japan is now Canada's fourth best customer.[12] Mainland China may offer only sporadic and unpredictable prospects for a variety of products but increasing grain and wood fibre sales are always a possibility and, as noted, China was Canada's sixth biggest customer in 1970.

A perceptive student of the Pacific, Lorne Kavic, points to the diversity of opportunities which may exist outside of China in the Pacific area for Canada:

... opportunities for export of a great variety of manufactures are expanding rapidly with the development of countries like Malaysia, Thailand, the Philippines, and Indonesia, with the increasing sophistication of Australia's import requirements, and with movements towards the liberalization of import controls in New Zealand and Japan. These developments, coupled with the efforts of most of the countries of the region to diversify their export markets and sources of imports, present the Canadian trader with exciting opportunities. And there is the additional possibility that large bulk ocean carriers, containerization, superports like Roberts Bank, and unit trains could enhance prospects of Canada becoming a "land bridge," linking the Pacific and Atlantic shipping lanes. The potential has provoked visions that the Pacific rim area will become Canada's greatest single trading partner, larger even than the United States, and that the Pacific economies will have as profound an effect on Canada's second century as the development of trade in the Atlantic community had on its first.[13]

[11] Lorne Kavic, "Canada And the Pacific: Prospects And Challenges," *Behind the Headlines* (Canadian Institute of International Affairs, May, 1970), p. 4.
[12] Canada's exports to Australia reached $197.7 million in 1970. Note 1, *ibid.*, p. 202.
[13] Kavic, *ibid.*

Yet, Canada cannot be complacent about Pacific trade opportunities. As Kavic points out:

> The grain-grower must contend with peculiarities of diet, world surpluses, extensive price-cutting by other producing countries, and new milling processes that require a lower proportion of Canada's high-quality wheat. The mining industry must acknowledge that the mineral wealth of many countries is being tapped by Japanese industry in accordance with a deliberate policy of avoiding excessive dependence upon any single source. The forest industry faces growing competition from local and other external suppliers, especially in the important Australian and Japanese markets. The manufacturer must contend with restrictive regulations in securing better access to the booming Japanese market, local efforts to stimulate secondary industries, and vigorous competition from European, American, Australian, and Japanese suppliers.[14]

Yet considerable substance remains in the assertion that Canada has become increasingly involved in the Pacific at various levels. In addition to Canada's recognition of the People's Republic of China, and the obvious trade increases in the last decade, Kavic lists many forms of involvement:

> Expenditure by the department on Pacific trade promotion, which totalled just $88,000 in 1968, was nearly doubled in 1969, with allocations of $165,000; Canada also participated in trade fairs in Australia, New Zealand, and Japan, and sent an observer to the Canton Trade Fair. Increased security for Canadian exporters is now available with the replacement, on 1 October 1969, of the 25-year-old Export Credits Insurance Corporation by an Export Development Corporation possessed of more flexible powers and twice as much capital with which to insure, guarantee, and finance Canadian exports in almost any area of activity.

> Provincial governments are demonstrating recognition of the advantages which could accrue from promotional efforts. Ontario announced in July 1969 that it intended to establish a trade and development office in Tokyo – its fourteenth overseas but the first in the Pacific. Alberta is considering establishment of a trade promotion office in Tokyo during 1970, possibly in conjunction with

[14] *Ibid.*, pp. 4-5.

Saskatchewan and Manitoba, and British Columbia may also set up a trade mission in Japan.

Canadian banks have moved energetically to service expanding trade (and investment) flows between Canada and its Pacific neighbours ... The British Columbia forest industry is active in promotional and sales work in the South Pacific and the Far East. Seaboard Lumber Sales and the promotion-oriented Council of Forest Industries of British Columbia represent about thirty companies in Australia, and MacMillan Bloedel maintains sales offices in Australia and Hong Kong. Canadian mining companies seem to be relatively well served by local subsidiaries and agents and by the nature of the trade which permits the despatch of missions as the occasion demands and the utilization of Vancouver-based Japanese trading company offices and visiting Japanese businessmen.

.... The late 1960's also witnessed a steadily increasing flow of Japanese money into extractive and manufacturing industries centred in British Columbia and Alberta. An Australian transportation firm has recently made a successful takeover bid for Gill Interprovincial Lines Limited of Vancouver. The scope of these investments cannot be accurately tabulated, but Japanese investments probably exceed $100 million, South-east Asian Chinese may have as much as $50 million, invested or on deposit in Canada, and the Australian takeover of Gill will involve about $4 million. Although Australia and New Zealand will not likely provide other than sporadic and small amounts of capital in future, Japan is expected to invest heavily in extractive industries oriented to meet the demands of its home industries, and on an increasing but more limited basis in secondary industries in order to exploit the Canadian and United States markets. It is possible that such investments may total some $500 million in British Columbia by 1975, and perhaps as high as $1 billion in all of Canada by that date . . .[15]

The skills and experience of various Canadian engineering and technological enterprises can become useful to Pacific nations. Canadian experience in the planning and construction of harbours and ports for example can be, and already is, of considerable value to such nations as Indonesia, Malaysia, and South Korea. The same

[15] *Ibid.*, p. 5.

may be true, for example, for Canadian experience in the development of nuclear energy for peaceful uses. There may also be some immediate prospects for sales of more finished goods to Japan (quality meat, processed foods, fur garments, and some machinery).

The idea of the Pacific as a "new west" for Canadian trade cannot therefore be dismissed solely as a rhetorical flourish. The Pacific has become one of the genuine new dimensions of Canadian external policy during this decade, yet the government of Canada could do much to accelerate the trend, and this will be discussed at the end of this chapter.

CANADIAN TRADE WITH WESTERN EUROPE

Of all the imponderables in Canadian trade in the 1970's, Canada's exports to Britain and the countries of Western Europe must rank very high. The historic Canadian instinct to increase trade with these countries remains. The White Paper notes that:

> The maintenance of an adequate measure of economic and political independence in the face of American power and influence is a problem Canada shares with the European nations, and in dealing with the problem there is at once an identity of interest and an opportunity for fruitful cooperation.

Yet considerable obstacles present themselves in European-Canadian trade. Examples specifically mentioned in the White Paper are: tariffs set by the EEC on a number of industrial materials of interest to Canada (aluminum and barley for example), limited access to EEC agricultural markets (at present the EEC is selling surpluses, with the aid of subsidies, to outside markets in competition with Canadian exports – wheat and other cereals especially). The EEC is developing a network of preferential arrangements with Mediterranean and African countries which, in the words of the White Paper, "could prejudice Canadian interests and which generally detract from the multilateral trading system developed with difficulty over the past two decades." On top of this, Canada's rate of increase of exports to Britain has been declining for most of the 1960's (although it revived to $1.48 billion in 1970[16] because of shifts in that country's trade policies. Although, as noted, probably up to as much as 28 per cent of Canadian exports to Britain will be further disturbed by the entry of Britain

[16] *Ibid.*, Note 1, p. 20.

to the Common Market into the EEC). Canada's share of imports and exports with East or West Europe has dropped in the past decade, and the merchandise surplus, traditionally held with Western Europe, has been falling since 1964. The surplus revived somewhat in 1970 as exports to the EEC rose from $850 million to $1.2 billion.

Yet, the White Paper adds, in 1968 continental Europe was, for the first time, a major market for new security issues of Canadian borrowers, and it notes that there was some direct participation by Canadian companies in European industry, adding that "Canada's current financial relationship with the United States requires that further growth in such participation generally be financed for the time being by borrowing in Europe." Canada's interest in France and in French-speaking Europe, for cultural reasons, may also improve chances for trade with France and the Common Market, although not too much evidence of this is forthcoming as yet. (Canada's trade with France was almost in balance at about the $158 million level in 1970. In the first eight months of 1971 Canada was running a deficit with $103,214,000 exports and $133,448,000 imports.)[17] To keep Canadian business and financial institutions interested in expanding in Western Europe, and to keep them up to date on market developments, the federal government will increase representation in national capitals, especially in Brussels where more emphasis on consultation with the European Community will be made. More specialized promotion efforts will be made in all Western European countries. In fact, Liberal MP Paul St. Pierre recently argued that Canadian industry must become less timid about the EEC market. His cautious note of optimism is worth quoting because it epitomizes the traditional Canadian attitude to European trade:

> True, for internal political reasons, [the EEC] will continue to protect the European farm and the European farm voter. They have a complex but highly efficient method of taking from their industrial profits to subsidize European agriculture and this they intend to continue. Canadian agriculture can take little cheer.

> The Eurocrats do insist that Canadian raw material can be taken in quantity, particularly since Europe has to buy much of this somewhere outside the EEC border anyway. And the market for manufactured goods, they said, increases as West Europe's pros-

---

[17] House of Commons, *Debates*, 1971, p. 9954.

perity moves ever upward. (Per capita GNP in the EEC was $2,045 in 1968, well behind the United States' $4,382 but well ahead of that of most of the world.)

(In 12 years, EEC's GNP rose 76 per cent, the United States' 62 per cent, Britain's 39 per cent.)

Our Canadian representatives on our diplomatic mission to EEC made much the same report to us.

"We tend too much to talk about the common tariff wall that surrounded EEC," said one spokesman. "The fact is that their tariff wall ranges from low to moderate on most goods. Generally, it's lower than our own tariff walls at home. . . ."

What discourages the Canadian team is an apparent lack of initiative by a large portion of the Canadian business community. Last year [1970] Canada increased her sales of manufactured goods in the United States. Our sales to EEC remained the same.

"Why is it," said the Canadian spokesman, "we can compete with American secondary industry within the States, but we seem to think we can't compete with American industry selling into Europe?"

Canada holds a mere 2.5 per cent of EEC's $40 billion annual imports – a poor position for one of the world's main trading nations. Both the Europeans and our own overseas representatives are convinced we could do better and should try harder.[18]

THE OPENING TO LATIN AMERICA

Canada's exports to, and imports from, Latin America have more than quadrupled since the Second World War, but the Latin American (excluding the Caribbean) share of total Canadian exports is only 3.5 per cent and is not increasing as rapidly as trade growth to other areas of the world. Moreover, the number of commodities that re-emerge as Canadian exports to Latin America have been limited in number and type. Also, there are institutional obstacles to the facilitation of trade with Latin America. To date, there is inadequate direct and continuing Canadian contact with governments through regional

[18] Paul St. Pierre, "Industry Too Timid in E.E.C. Market," *Canadian Business*, February, 1971, pp. 39-40, 42.

and international organizations such as the Latin America Free Trade Area, and the Central American Common Market, and other sub-groupings. A severe shortage of foreign exchange in Latin America makes export credits and insurance facilities vital in order to ease the sale of capital equipment and bulk commodities. Finally, there is the need for Latin Americans to find diversified markets for their own secondary industry and this involves high external tariffs and other forms of protection.

Imports to Canada from Latin America are limited in range, mainly petroleum and petroleum products, and coffee, despite the absence of Canadian restrictions on Latin American products. The Foreign Policy White Paper states quite bluntly that "in the last analysis, the level of sales of Latin American goods in Canada will depend on the promotional efforts of the Latin Americans themselves."

In its attempt to choose an appropriate emphasis for Canada with regard to Latin America, an accent on trade and investment with political, cultural, and scientific relations evolving on an *ad hoc* basis has been rejected by the White Paper as an "inadequate response to the potentialities of the Latin American relationship in the years ahead." Yet Canada also fully rejects a fully multilateral approach to these fields, especially an approach that would involve full membership in the OAS. Instead, Canada has opted for a systematic strengthening of links through nation-to-nation programs in the economic, cultural, and political spheres, while at the same time, to quote the White Paper, "drawing closer to the Inter-American System and some of its organizations without actually becoming a member of the OAS." (Canada became a "Permanent Observer" of the OAS in early 1972.)

The OAS membership issue has been a long-standing one in Canada. Since 1965 there has been more interest in Latin America but less interest in the OAS. The recent White Paper again posed the problem, when it noted that new members (Barbados, Jamaica, Trinidad, Tobago) are giving the organization a more "hemispheric character." Canada's reservations about OAS lie mainly with the substantial commitment this would mean financially and politically. Membership would mean, according to the White Paper, that "Canada would increasingly be expected to determine its policies and practices with regard to economic relations with other countries of the hemisphere through consultations in this forum." It would mean a tendency "at least initially, to restrict Canadian freedom of action in development

assistance matters, since . . . the Inter-American Development Bank
. . . and other OAS development assistance programs could absorb most
available resources for a period of many years." Also, "the potential
obligation to apply political and economic sanctions against another
country by virtue of an affirmative vote of two-thirds of the members
is a difficult feature of the OAS from a Canadian point of view. . . .
This could limit the Canadian Government's freedom of action with
regard to a future security crisis in the hemisphere." The analysis
concludes that "Canada's direct interest in the political affairs of the
hemisphere is real but somewhat limited."

The Canadian view of Latin America seems to focus as much on
cultural opportunities as on economic or political ones. In fact, the
whole Trudeau approach to Latin America is exploratory. "Understanding" and "people-to-people relationships" seem to be of first
importance in order to, "discover what Canada's distinctive role
might be." For this reason, bilateral relationships are preferred to the
multilateral approach. The problems which Canada has experienced
with the slow rate of disbursement of funds by the Inter-American
Bank (arising from the difficulty of matching different procedures and
regulations), have further inhibited development efforts in the area,
and lend support to the bilateral emphasis.

THESE THREE ARENAS REVISITED

In examining these three regional arenas for Canadian trade, it appears
that Canada has only begun to link its study of them to strengthening
its manufacturing industries. Under the recent Export Market Development Program, $3 million was earmarked for "precontractural"
work for Canada's manufacturing industries (*Financial Post*, February 19, 1972, p. 3).

But if Canada wishes to emphasize more manufactured and processed exports, it must recognize that in the Pacific, it will have to
compete with three aggressive export traders, the Japanese, the Americans, and Australians; in Europe with the U.S.; and in Latin America, with the U.S. again. Evidence of Canadian aggressiveness in
promoting such exports in these regions even if it goes beyond preliminary promotion efforts, does not seem to come to grips with ambi-
tions for a labour-intensive industrial strategy, or with the readily
apparent competitive factors of the international marketplace, especially in the Pacific. An aggressive, imaginative attempt is necessary to
identify the skills and services that Pacific, Latin American, and Eu-

ropean nations lack and which Canada could supply. Such an approach might also help to orient the priorities of Canada's research, development, and education strategies. For example, Canada's work in marine research, transportation, harbour development, research, planning, and engineering of its resources, could all be exported in the form of consulting and engineering services, prototype supplies, tool and die exports, etc., (services and products in which Canada is particularly strong), all leading to substantial markets. Canada is also clearly qualified, as the White Paper notes, to provide technical expertise in the fields of telecommunications, grain storage facilities, hydroelectric equipment, pulp and paper machinery, specialized aircraft, subway, road, and rail equipment, nuclear reactors, airport construction, aerial surveys, and educational equipment. Identification of capabilities and potential, combined with a freeing of more export opportunities for Canadian subsidiaries is, and will be, imperative.

To pursue all these options is in essence to pursue more vigorously the conventional Canadian trade strategy of relying on about two-thirds of Canadian exports going to the U.S. together with *ad hoc* attempts to develop exports outside of the U.S. to decrease this dependence, at least incrementally. This strategy, if vigorously pursued, might afford some important increases in Canada's exports outside of the U.S. Yet some Canadians are generating at least three fundamentally different perspectives on the whole strategy itself and they deserve at least a brief introduction.

1. There are always those, (notably British Columbia's Premier W. A. C. Bennett in 1971), who call for an end to the insistence that non-U.S. markets should be pursued as a "counterveiling force" to U.S. trade. This argument is that Canada should aim primarily for a "free trade common market between Canada and the United States." (*Globe and Mail*, November 8, 1971, pp. 1, 2.) This view is evident in the Canadian Chamber of Commerce, in government circles in a number of other provinces and to some extent in Ottawa as well.[19]

[19] For academic studies on the costs and benefits of free trade between the U.S. and Canada see Ronald J. Wonnacott and Paul Wonnacott, *Free Trade Between the United States And Canada: The Potential Economic Effects* (Cambridge, Mass.: 1967); Roy A. Mathews, *Industrial Viability In A Free Trade Economy* (published for the Private Planning Association of Canada by the University of Toronto Press, Toronto, 1971); and various studies by the Canadian American Committee published in Montreal and Washington and listed along with other bibliographical suggestions in Mathews, *op. cit.*, pp. 141-144.

2. A small but growing number of Canadians are beginning to glimpse the congruence between Canada's problem of dependence on resource exports and its difficulties in generating exports of end-products with the problems of a number of many developing (if less wealthy) countries. Canada and a number of developing countries are facing the problem of having to export more resources to pay for the same amount of end-products imported from industrialized countries. (Eighty per cent of the foreign-exchange earnings of developing countries comes from exports of primary commodities.[20]) Therefore Canada, according to this logic, might be wise to consider initiating more discussions with developing countries to begin a concerted re-examination of their common problems. In the opinion of one observer, Andrew Carvely, the editor of *The Nonaligned Third World Annual*, "Canada might well evolve into a new prominent international position leading the resource-rich nations of Latin America, the Middle East, Africa and even some Asian and European nations toward a force, the impact of which would dwarf Asia, including Japan."[21]

3. Finally there is the school of thought that argues that any of these strategies (including the conventional one) cannot be pursued effectively by any Canadian government as long as all of the disincentives against making such strategies work continue to be sown into Canada's industrial structure by the foreign ownership of its economy. To some extent this view is supported in a private paper produced for the Cabinet on foreign investment and subsequently published by the *Canadian Forum*, December, 1971 (the leaked Gray Report on foreign ownership). It is the premise of this school that foreign ownership of key sectors of Canada's economy must be lessened before any strategy emphasizing either less dependence on trade with the U.S. or (its opposite) free trade could be workable. To try to alter present patterns without lifting the "dead-hand" of foreign ownership on Canada's export performance [according to this argument] is to pursue a Quixotic policy. This is not confined to the Waffle wing of the NDP but appears to a lesser degree as well in the October, 1971, analysis of the Science Council of Canada.

It is difficult to predict how important these three radically alterna-

---

[20] These figures are contained in Trade Minister Jean Luc Pepin's speech, November 6, 1970, "Canada's Trade with Developing Countries," p. 4.
[21] See his "Canada: Forgotten Center of Power," *Globe and Mail*, November 4, 1971, p. 7.

tive strategies will be in the 1970's but there should be no mistaking that they arise in part out of a growing and increasingly widespread concern about the efficacy of the conventional strategy.

Chapter 6

Canadian-American Economic Relations: Current Issues

The considerable disparity in size and structure between the U.S. and Canadian economies, and the diversity of the economic relations between them have forced the two countries to perceive their mutual economic problems in fundamentally different ways. As we have seen, the United States is by far Canada's most important trading partner (consuming 65 per cent of Canada's exports in 1970). But U.S. reliance on Canada for its trade, while sizeable, is less pronounced. It is vital to recognize, therefore, that economic issues of great importance to Canada are most often handled in a multilateral context by the American government. In other words, the impact of an American policy decision on Canada may not be considered any more seriously than its impact on a number of other countries likely to be affected. Indeed, frequently, (even before August 15, 1971) American relations with a third country have determined policies that affected Canadian interests. For example, even before the 1971 U.S. surtax imposition, in an attempt to amend what was considered a disadvantageous trade position with Japan, the United States reinforced the administration of its anti-dumping laws, with some pernicious consequences for Canada. Another example is the U.S. Tariff Commission's 1970 report recommending retention of tariff exemptions for re-entry of U.S.-made parts assembled abroad. This clearly benefited Canadian manufacturers, (in 1969 they exported to the United States $269 million worth of goods that included $83 million of components that originated in the United States and re-entered duty free). Yet the exemptions were jeopardized by AFL-CIO pressure directed not against Canada but against the number of factories set up in Mexico, Formosa, and South Korea that have been using cheap labour to assemble parts re-entering without duty.

The obvious remedy for such situations has been for Canada to establish its status as a special case in those areas of vital interest directly affected by American economic policy. In wartime and early post-war years, for example, Canadian importers were assisted in the purchase of scarce but vital commodities by the Hyde Park principle of sharing adopted by the two countries in 1941. Since then the Canadian government has treated this concept of "sharing" gingerly, because it smacked of "integration" and would have given the United States an undesirable bargaining advantage in the conduct of economic relations. Yet, in certain areas, Canada has sought various forms of "special status," for example: with respect to privileged access for certain Canadian exports such as crude oil; for exemption from the U.S. Interest Equalization Tax; in Defence Production Sharing Agreements; in modified free trade in automobiles, and so on. Even so, Canada's special interests, usually recognized as such by the United States because they coincided with the important interests of that country, have on several occasions been overlooked in Washington. Two examples of such oversight are the original blanket imposition of the Interest Equalization Tax in 1963, and the Immigration Act of 1968 (now being amended) that so reduced the quota of Canadian immigrants into the United States as to make company personnel transfer between the two countries extremely difficult.

It is difficult, however, to identify the extent of "special treatment" and the lack of it in all the economic dimensions of U.S.-Canadian relations. The subject matter of Canadian-American economic relations is so vast and varied, covering such problems as the alignment of wheat prices, the administration of customs duties (which has displayed an incredible degree of arbitrariness on the part of both countries), the continued export of Canadian softwood lumber which is threatened by western lumber interests in the United States, the effort to secure an exemption for Canadian-produced books from the manufacturing clause of the United States Copyright Law which inhibits their importation, and the annual problem of commodity trade between two countries with different growing seasons.

Three particular issues rank highest on the agenda of Canadian-

American negotiations in the 1970's and they deserve at least an introductory examination here. They are: natural resources, trade and capital movements, and ownership of Canadian industry.

NATURAL RESOURCES

The issue of "resource sharing" is not new to U.S.-Canadian relations. Five provinces – New Brunswick, Quebec, Ontario, Manitoba, and British Columbia – have hydro-electric power hook-ups with American states. Most attention, however, has been directed to the subject of Canadian exports of crude oil to the United States which were breaking all records in early 1970, and were then cut back by presidential decision. To many Canadians, the decision appeared to be a deliberate effort to force Canada to agree to a free market in energy resources (a recommendation by the President's task force on oil imports headed by George Schultz).

Canada is unique among nations in being both an importer and an exporter of oil. It is an exporter by virtue of a favourable quota, originally granted by the Eisenhower Administration on the grounds that Canada could be considered a militarily secure source of supply. The American version of a continental energy policy, or free market (similar to the Schultz report), assures the United States of an even greater dependability of supply, by enabling western Canadian oil to be shipped to Quebec and the Maritimes, which now receive their supplies from sources judged insecure (Venezuela and, to a much lesser extent, the Middle East). If an east-west oil pipeline, which the Canadian oil industry considers uneconomic, were to be built, this would remove the temptation for Canada to enter the American market to compete for limited oil supplies in the case of an international crisis which might cut off present overseas sources. Yet, "security of supply" is a highly flexible concept as President Nixon demonstrated by gradually relaxing restrictions on the import of Canadian oil, considered "insecure" by the task force, in late 1970. He was apparently forced to do this by both fear of a domestic shortage, and the desire to stabilize, or possibly drive down, oil prices in his fight against inflation. On top of this, the Canada-U.S. Cabinet Committee on Economic Affairs, meeting in November 1970, reached an informal agreement for future full and unimpeded access to U.S. markets of Canadian crude oil and petroleum products, surplus to Canadian commercial and security requirements.[1] Canada, therefore,

[1] Joint Communique, November 24, 1970.

appears close to its objective of an open market for oil exports without the commitments required by the "continental" approach. Total concentration of exports in one market is not without an aspect of dependence, especially considering the political influence of the Amercan "oil lobby" which aims at higher prices and expanded domestic production. (However, the Canadian government, following the recommendation of the National Energy Board on November 19, 1971, has decided to avoid this dependence in the case of natural gas, in its agreement with the Board that no surplus of natural gas exists for export until more reserves are found. According to the Energy Board, it appears that Canadian demands for natural gas "are increasing much more quickly than previously foreseen even as recently as August 1970," when permission was last given for a large export of natural gas.)

It should be noted that Canada's "National Energy Policy," requiring the country to be supplied by both domestic and imported supplies of oil, is not without social and political implications. The imported oil is consumed in politically volatile Quebec and the economically depressed Maritimes. Given the present world price structure, imported oil is cheaper than domestic, and this is reflected in the prices of refined products, such as automobile gasoline. It remains to be seen whether the recent success of the Organization of Petroleum Exporting Countries, in demanding higher revenues from the oil companies, will result in higher prices for Canada's imported oil that effectively remove the price differential for the eastern Canadian consumer.

The growing realization by some Americans of the potential shortages of oil, natural gas, hydro-electric power and, potentially, even of water, in the United States has focussed attention on Canada's ability to alleviate these shortages. This realization extends far beyond government bureaucracies. Resource policy has become a pre-eminently political, not technical, issue. It is widely advertized in Canada as Canada's opportunity to deal with the Americans from a position of strength, or even as an opportunity to right the long-time imbalance of Canadian-American economic relations.[2] Canada's capacities and American needs are so often mentioned that to summarize them now is to reiterate the commonplace. Here, based on Canada's National Energy Board estimates in 1970, are three startling comparisons:

[2] See for example the remarks of a former conservative Cabinet Minister, Alvin Hamilton, "A National Energy Policy for Canada," York University, November 24, 1970.

1. Canadian consumption of water is not likely to go higher than 6 per cent of total capacity by 1990; American demand will likely match its supply around 1985 to 1990.

2. Canada appears to have about 500 billion barrels of oil reserves, giving it a comfortable cushion for at least the next century (these calculations may be modest, given the recent Panarctic discoveries in the Arctic, announced February 24, 1972). Since the United States cannot supply its own needs now, it must turn somewhere, and Canada seems to be the obvious direction.

3. While Canada probably has sufficient hydro-electric capacity to meet domestic demand to the end of the century, parts of the United States must already face the prospect of "brown-outs" during the summer.

   In order to join Canadian capacity to U.S. needs, American authorities have suggested a "continental energy policy." Any so-called continental energy policy would probably include natural gas, oil, electrical power, coal and nuclear energy, and later, water resources. American industry would have permanent access to these resources and a guarantee of no interference with future supply regardless of whatever needs Canada may develop in the future. It should be made clear, however, as intimated earlier, that quite apart from the lack of flexibility involved for Canada in becoming a committed supplier of U.S. energy, the new mood of Canada at present renders impossible any selling arrangement that would give the United States the appearance of such unilateral control over Canadian natural resources. In line with this emphasis, the present Canadian government has made it clear that it favours some sales to the United States, subject to conditions that meet ecological imperatives, and after the establishment of amounts surplus to Canadian needs.

   The mood of opposition to any sort of "continentalism" now includes those who question the wisdom of any sale of energy whatsoever to the United States. Anti-Americanism motivates some nationalists in their disapproval of energy deals with the United States. They have no wish to see Canadian energy powering the military-industrial machine that fights the Vietnam war and exploits the rest of the world. James Laxer, a spokesman for the nationalist and most socialist wing of the New Democratic Party (the Waffle Group), has even suggested that Canada should leave untapped her supplies of natural gas until tanker export abroad becomes feasible.[3] Since the Waffle Group has fairly ambitious social objectives, including widespread public ownership and restructuring of the economy, they take all the more seriously any implied inhibitions on Canada's future freedom of action resulting from a resource deal with the U.S.

Yet Canadian concern permeates a much wider spectrum of political opinion. It ranges from those who hesitate to commit all Canada's surplus resource eggs to the American basket because other nations might need these resources, to those who want more Canadian processing, to those who demand tougher conservation safeguards and finally, to those who worry about the erratic pattern of U.S. markets. (The story of the Canadian uranium mining industry vividly substantiates the latter fear, as it was largely built on American purchases. When the U.S. Government's needs declined in 1959, it started to reduce purchases of Canadian uranium in order to maintain orders with American mines. This resulted in the virtual destruction of one Ontario mining town, Elliot Lake, and caused much bitterness in Canada.)

In short, energy nationalists, although a minority, are nonetheless an unusually potent force precisely because the topic of energy is one field in which public opinion is most favourable to their line of argument. Indeed, the ambiguities involved in energy questions probably increase, not decrease, the attractiveness of the position of the energy nationalists. The sense of sailing headlong into an uncharted sea provokes caution, not precipitate action. There is uncertainty about the employment effects and effects on the Canadian dollar of unprocessed energy export to the U.S. since resource industries are more capital than labour intensive. American corporations, let alone Japanese corporations, involved in the Canadian oil and natural gas industry have not found it in their interests to greatly expand refining and processing operations in Canada. If Canada does not insist on more processing, the long struggle to diversify manufacturing may be conclusively lost, and the country will, in effect, have moved the terms of trade against itself. There is, then, real uncertainty as to whether surrender of some Canadian control of resources actually would bring the greatest economic benefit. There is also uncertainty about the demands Canada itself will place on its energy resources in the future. The National Energy Board's calculations on natural gas

[3] See James Laxer, *The Energy Poker Game* (Toronto: New Press, 1970).

reserves in 1971 point to a near equality in Canadian domestic needs and supply. In the case of other kinds of energy, not only are detailed inventories lacking in some cases, but the possibility of large petroleum and natural gas discoveries on the Atlantic Shelf or in the Arctic makes accurate assessment of "surplus for export" extremely difficult.

The impact of large-scale exploitation of Canadian resources on the ecological environment also acts as a restraint on action. For example, will the Canadian Government be able to enforce the regulations appropriate to oil exploration in the Arctic on a multinational firm that can easily switch its operation to a more hospitable jurisdiction? In 1971 this concern focussed on the proposed shipment of Alaskan oil from Valdes to the Pacific Coast of the United States, with fears of disastrous oil spills near the coast of British Columbia running very high. On the subject of Canada's water reserves, McGill University geographer, Trevor Lloyd, has suggested that because of low precipitation in the North, much of Canada's fresh water cannot be considered as a *renewable* resource to be bartered away.

All these concerns combine in the demand that Canada maintain tight control over her energy resources through explicit national policies and priorities. Fortifying these demands is the undoubted fact that maintenance of Canada's heritage has become something of a shibboleth, the ultimate symbol of sovereignty in an age when concern about the ecology has become so widespread in North America.

Yet all this considered, it may be that Canada's willingness to supply the United States with sources of energy may not be as major a factor in American concerns over their emerging possible "energy gap" as Canadians think. Perhaps it ought to be but does not appear to be. For example, a September 1, 1970, background study for the Joint Economic Committee of the U.S. Congress "The Economy, Energy, and the Environment," emphasizes only two sets of factors in its overview of this problem: the number of different patterns of U.S. energy *markets* which could emerge in the future; and the host of financial, environmental and technological assumptions which have to be met before making any projections about these markets to the year 2000. No mention was made of Canada's attitudes towards energy export anywhere in the report.

Here is the essence of the report's emphasis. First, there is a guarded optimism about the emergence of new forms of energy:

Given a dynamic, changing pattern in energy demand and supply, one can understand the different opinions about the future of the U.S. energy market shown by various forecasters. Although nuclear power supplies only a minute part of present energy demands, some forecasters expect uranium and thorium will become the largest single source of energy for the nation within the next three decades.[4]

The study also emphasizes the changing prospects for more familiar forms of energy:

Given our larger resources of coal and oil shale, and the technological prospects for converting them into fluid fuels, the dominance of the petroleum-like fuels is not likely to continue for the rest of this century. For the more distant future, there are hopes that certain forms of hydrogen atoms, which are present in nature, can be used as fuel in the fusion process, which in essence could provide an inexhaustible supply.

As for the future, the Office of Science and Technology recently released results of a study made for it by the Battelle Memorial Institute which compared many recent forecasts of energy supply and demand. . . .

All of the existing projections analyzed by the Institute estimate that oil (including natural gas liquids) will continue to be the Nation's largest source of energy through the year 2000. Natural gas, excluding liquid fuels made from natural gas, is expected to continue to be the second largest source of energy. Of three projections for both nuclear power and coal at the end of the century, one estimates that coal will provide slightly more energy than nuclear, another estimates just the opposite and one foresees a large margin for a nuclear. At the moment, the Federal Power Commission and the Atomic Energy Commission favour the second estimate.

Hydro-electric power is expected to continue to grow, but to be of decreasing relative importance and to supply the smallest amount of any of the commercial energy sources in the year 2000. Nuclear

[4] U.S. Government Printing Office, Washington D.C., *The Economy, Energy And the Environment: A Background Study Prepared for the Use of the Joint Economic Committee Congress of the United States*, September 1, 1970, pp. 4,5.

generation is expected to exceed hydro-electric generation sometime between the years 1975-80.[5]

Apart from these perspectives on markets, which make it clear that there will be considerable American consumption of petroleum-like fuels to the end of the century, the report is strangely unconcerned about Canadian willingness to supply these fuels. Its discussion of possible shortages for the electrical industry, typifies this:

> Looking ahead for the next two decades and projecting the recent growth and demand for electricity, the supply of fuel materials of oil, coal and uranium, but probably not for natural gas, will be adequately available in deposits accessible to the United States.[6]

A similar assessment appeared in the November 15, 1971, issue of the *Oil and Gas Journal*. It includes, however, a warning about rising costs:

> The United States of America is not running out of energy. Despite the welter of surveys, studies, and reports of an "energy crisis" we have within our borders, on reliable call, enough hydrocarbon resources to keep our economy moving for generations to come.

> The United States is, however, running out of cheap energy. The same can be said for the world at large. . . . The cost of America's energy is rising because all of the new ingredients being brought into the mix come in at sharply higher prices.

TRADE AND CAPITAL MOVEMENTS

Since almost 72 per cent of Canada's imports in 1970 came from the United States and 65 per cent of Canadian exports were purchased in the U.S., Canadians who are concerned about this reliance on the U.S. market will naturally take satisfaction in seeing new trade markets open up in other parts of the world. As noted in the previous chapter, it is a professed aim of the Trudeau Government to try to lessen Canadian dependence on the American market by developing new trading links with, for example, the nations of the Pacific. At present no one other nation takes as much as 10 per cent of Canada's sales abroad, therefore maintaining and extending access to the

[5] *Ibid.*, p. 9.
[6] *Ibid.*

American market has been a recurring theme of Canadian economic policy. To do this Canada has tried to discourage the development of protectionist blocks in the U.S. and elsewhere, and applauds U.S. efforts that champion free trade. This explains Canadian enthusiasm for the formation of GATT (General Agreement on Trade and Tariffs) and Canada's careful efforts to ensure American membership. In the 1970's it is obvious once more that it is in establishing decreasingly protective international standards of commercial behaviour that Canada hopes to restrain protectionist sentiment in the U.S. Such sentiment is always to be feared, not only for its effects on Canadian exports, but for the antagonism it could arouse among other trading partners. An economy as heavily dependent on trade as Canada's (20 per cent of the Canadian GNP is exported) could be mortally wounded by a mounting wave of trade protectionism. In fact, within months of the August, 1971, announcement of the 10 per cent U.S. surtax on imports, the Canadian Trade Minister announced that the Canadian Government would open a new offensive for more liberalized trade in the western world.

What also deserves special attention from observers of U.S.-Canadian relations is the relationship between bilateral trade, and the movement of American capital into Canada and within Canada. The standard pattern of the postwar years has been that of a Canadian current account deficit with the United States compensated by a capital account surplus. An important anomaly accounting for this capital account surplus is that Canadians, who are among the highest savers in the world, have considered themselves in the past to be unable to fulfill their own capital requirements. Canada has thought this way even though, counting foreign reserves accumulation as a capital export, Canada was a net exporter of capital in 1970. (Speeches by provincial premiers indicate that most of them believe that the need for selected amounts of foreign capital will continue into the 1970's as well.) This domestic capital deficiency has been variously attributed to the lack of a merchant banking facility able to provide venture capital at medium terms; to the inherent cautiousness of Canadian investors; to the use of Canadian savings for American takeovers instead of for new enterprise; to the high Canadian investment outside of Canada; and to the undoubted magnitude of Canada's capital needs. To argue that Canada has been capital poor may therefore be incorrect; it may be more accurate to say that it is in the *organization* of massive investments for large resource and industrial developments that New

York and Chicago have outdone Toronto and Montreal. For example, one perceptive Canadian economist explains the aggressiveness of the multinational corporation, and the diffidence of the Canadian public and private sector towards high risk ventures this way:

> ... normal commercial ventures imply a quite different economic setting and different rules of the game from development ventures sponsored by the government. Canadian business may not feel at home with the ground rules, different modes of financing, and higher levels of risk which are inherent in developing the poorer regions of this country. The aim of government – to create employment opportunities – may not coincide with their own general aims of an orderly and controlled expansion of their operations geared to normal profit opportunities and unencumbered by novel administrative relations to government agencies ... Why should foreign, particularly American, firms feel entirely at home in this setting and operate quite easily under a different set of "rules of the game?" The answer lies in recognizing the character of the multinational corporation, whose experience lies primarily in establishing new ventures in developing areas around the world. They are equipped to assess the unusual risks involved in the financial, managerial, and economic side of the operation and to cope with these problems accordingly. Their talents, however, do not come cheaply and we must appreciate fully the price we have to pay for foreign investment.[7]

The efficiency of the Canadian capital market, and its willingness and capacity to undertake risks and to support entrepreneurship, also emerged as a concern in the unauthorized version of the federal government's report on foreign ownership. This report expressed concern with the extent to which Canada relies upon Canadian financial institutions to help finance new and generally more risky economic activity and the extent to which foreign sources finance these ventures. "If Canada relies heavily on foreign sources, this would clearly reduce domestic capacity to control the economic environment. It would also likely reduce possibilities of increased Canadian ownership."[8] The report goes on:

---

[7] A. Rotstein in his preface to P. Mathias, *Forced Growth* (Toronto: 1971), pp. x, xi.

[8] *The Canadian Forum*, December 1971.

The evidence available suggests that Canadians finance a much smaller proportion of the growth in productive capacity in Canada than the volume of Canadian savings would permit. This reflects many factors.

Firstly, many foreign controlled enterprises are already in Canada and able to finance expansion out of internally generated funds.

Secondly, new firms enter Canada for reasons exogenous to Canadian capacities in financing, technology or management. For instance, the foreigner may find it profitable to exploit his product or technology in Canada or to obtain Canadian natural resources for supply assuredness and no barriers exist to his doing so.

Thirdly, foreigners take on projects which are judged to be too risky by Canadians. The foreigner's perception of the risk in many cases, however, is different than the Canadian's. The real risk is simply much smaller for him for one reason or another – because an export market is assured, a tax advantage is available, the investment constitutes a smaller part of his investment portfolio, he has greater experience in the business, his cost of money is cheaper or whatever. These are all reasons which help to explain the reason why Canadian savings are not channelled into indigenous development to as great an extent as is possible.[9]

Also central to trade and capital movements between the two countries is the emerging problem of the slow growth of the manufacturing sector in Canada, particularly after noting the strength of the Canadian manufacturing sector in the early 1960's. Omond Solandt, the Chairman of the Science Council of Canada has argued, similarly to Chapter 4, that Canada, in the 1970's "is in real danger of becoming a post-industrial state that does not have the industrial base to sustain its economy. . . . Investments in more labour-intensive activities in secondary manufacturing – and particularly in activities which use larger numbers of well-trained people – might well be better for Canada," (*Toronto Star*, June 30, 1971).

A key part of any consideration of Canada's manufacturing sector

[9] See Edward Safarian, "The Web of Repercussions," in Stephen Clarkson, ed., *An Independent Foreign Policy for Canada?* (Toronto: McClelland and Stewart, 1968); and Walter Gordon, *A Choice for Canada* (Toronto: McClelland and Stewart, 1966).

is the whole question of the Auto Pact. In 1970, automobiles and auto parts accounted for one-third of Canada's total manufactured shipments to the United States. (Newsprint is second, at 9 to 10 per cent.) It is perhaps instructive to recognize the motive for this pact. The initiatives began in the early sixties, with the aims of increasing production and employment in Canada, improving the balance of payments, and enabling Canadian producers of both parts and vehicles to achieve longer production runs and greater specialization with the consequent reduction in costs. The result of these efforts was the Canada-United States Automotive Agreement which was signed in January 1965, and which provided in essence for free trade in a wide range of new automotive products, including parts. So favourable has this been to some Canadian economic interests that some observers feel that the Americans must have extracted a heavy price for it, such as the Canadian contribution to the Cyprus Peace Force, or the exemption of *Time* and *Reader's Digest* from the Government's 1966 magazine legislation.[10] Whatever the validity of these hypotheses, there is no doubt that the effect of the Pact on the balance of payments has been an unpleasant surprise to American officials, thus heightening chagrin at their economic problems in general and the capital flow to Canada in particular.

The production commitments called for a minimum ratio of Canadian assembly to Canadian sales and a floor on the Canadian value – added in Canadian produced vehicles. Both are contained in an Annex to the Agreement. These were the key operative clauses. The purpose of these commitments was to prevent a migration of auto manufacturing from Canada where costs and prices were above U.S. levels. No time limit was ever specified for these safeguards and they have now become the cause of a major conflict of interpretation. When the development of production facilities in Canada began to exceed the commitments, U.S. authorities began work in the early 1970's to have them removed. The confusion over these commitments is a rather telling indication of the intimate, *ad hoc* manner in which Canadian-American relations have been conducted up to the present. It also raises questions about just how permanent are any so-called "structural shifts" which come from such work-sharing agreements.

A pamphlet entitled "Toward a More Realistic Appraisal of the Automotive Agreement," which the Canadian-American Committee

---

[10] See Kal Hosti, "The United States And Canada," in S. L. Spiegel and K. N. Waltz, *Conflict in World Politics* (Cambridge, Mass: 1971), pp. 389-394.

(a bilateral Chamber of Commerce, Labour, etc. group) published in 1970 as a response to American criticism of the Pact, argues that there is no convincing rationale behind present methods of evaluating it. It suggests that in the early 1970's assessments of the amount of cars to be produced in Canada were almost bound to be premature. "While the major U.S. firms understandably added their first large increments of new production facilities on the Canadian side after the Agreement was launched, their next major investments may well take place on the U.S. side, tending to arrest, if not to counterbalance, the movement of production to Canada during the past few years." Most assessments in the popular press in Canada are too narrowly focussed for intelligent assessment of the Pact, according to the Committee. It argues that the Canadians, in their emphasis on narrowing the gap between the value of Canadian production and the value of Canadian purchases, and Americans, by their obsession with their automotive trade balance, are both using very restricted criteria of judgement. The Committee would prefer to direct attention to the total effect on the economies of the two countries. This includes the effect on industries related to the automotive industry and the incredibly difficult question of what would have happened in the absence of the Agreement. Clearly the Committee was trying to smother a quarrel that could exacerbate the present problems of the relationship, by pleading the need for further research, yet it was also emphasizing some of the conceptual difficulties that are encountered in tackling problems of economic policy in the Canadian-American context.

Canada's current difficulties with the United States in the areas of trade and investment also have to be seen in relation to the American balance of payments which has steadily worsened during the 1960's. American authorities have claimed that a partial explanation to this deterioration lies in Canada's dependence on American capital, and that this dependence persuaded the U.S. to grant an exemption from the Interest Equalization Tax when it was initially proposed in 1963. The exemption may have been granted instead, however, because of the knowledge in Washington that the American balance of payments was being strengthened in the long run by its transactions with Canada, especially in the resource sector. Witness that the exemption was granted again in 1971 when the Interest Equalization Tax was reimposed. No *quid pro quo* was asked for despite the fact that Canada no longer needed the capital inflow to right a current account deficit with the U.S. This exemption has, therefore, been granted twice as was another, in March, 1968, after a Canadian exchange crisis stemming from the investment guidelines of the Johnson Administration. Canada may perhaps have helped to secure these exemptions by agreeing to put the best appearance on U.S. international accounts by carrying its U.S. dollar reserves not in short-term marketable securities, that is, U.S. Treasury Bills, but in special non-negotiable, longer-term paper. This is not a particularly onerous restriction, but one that Canadians of such divergent views as conservative W. Earle McLaughlin, President and Chairman of the Royal Bank of Canada, and Kari Levitt of McGill University, author of *Silent Surrender* (concerning Canada's surrender of its independence through accepting foreign investment), have both found particularly humiliating.

Finally, U.S. policy-makers in the 1970's are concerned about the deterioration in their trade balance with Canada. After decades of American trade surpluses with Canada, it appears that Canada emerged in 1970 with a surplus (although, according to preliminary indications, this surplus declined to only $245 million in 1971). The Auto Pact, the defence production sharing agreements, and growing Canadian oil exports were the major contributors to the surplus. Canada's foreign exchange reserves have climbed to a record level ($4.8 billion at the end of January 1971, $3 billion of which was in U.S. dollars). In December 1968, the governments in Washington and Ottawa agreed that Canada no longer needed to keep a ceiling on her reserves, but that the Canadian government should nonetheless exert its efforts to hold down Canadian borrowing in the United States. By 1972, however, this emphasis had lessened in Washington. U.S. efforts to increase its economic leverage in Canada centred on a strategy to increase Canada's imports of manufactured goods from the U.S., *and* to allow foreign investments to develop Canada's resources for export. (See U.S. Treasury Undersecretary Paul Volker's arguments, *Financial Post*, February 26, 1972, p. 6; and *Toronto Star*, March 6, 1972, p. 8.)

What can be tentatively observed from all this, however, is the hardening American attitude towards both capital outflow, the Auto Pact, and other trade questions, and this signals a new era in Canadian-American relations. A time of tougher bargaining and narrower emphasis on calculable interest is at hand. Canada's *Financial Post* (February 26, 1972, p. 6) has argued that the Volker strategy suggests a new "vassaldom" for Canada. It is not surprising that many Canadians suspect President Nixon's assurances that the U.S. does not seek a permanent trade surplus with Canada to be less than candid. It appears that acts of political will will probably be as vital as anything else. Before the Nixon economic message of August 15, 1971, and concomittant rumours of a U.S. "list of grievances against Canada" (*Chicago Tribune*, October 11, 1971, p. 1), it might have been guessed that the exercise of that will would probably have been primarily from Canada. In late 1971, however, the United States appeared to be exercising its will more forcibly than even Canadian diplomats in Washington ever expected and Canada's response has not been totally coherent. Since even the assumptions and tactics behind Canada's "conventional" trade and capital movements strategy are being attacked by the American emphasis on "repatriating" jobs from Canada, the Trudeau cabinet ministers were talking as if a restoration of even the "conventional" U.S.-Canadian relationship on trade and capital movements would be a relief, (see *Toronto Star*, December 2, 1971).

This tough exercise of will at high political levels is in contrast to U.S.-Canadian relations since World War II. For example, in a paper written at the end of the 1960's, based upon a number of interviews with senior career officials of the Canadian Departments of Finance, External Affairs, and Industry, Trade and Commerce, in October, 1969, a University of British Columbia political scientist, Kal Holsti, was able to suggest various inhibitions on both the U.S. and Canada from pressing either's power too far in their relations with each other. He explained this primarily by reference to the "diplomatic ethic and culture," between the two countries, not simply the "mutuality of interests" which exists between them. This ethic and culture helped to explain how agreements were reached "without wide publicity" and with a "mutual feeling of ease and frankness." He argued also that the "willingness of the agencies of one government to act in the interests of another (government)," the relative absence of "spillover of conflict from one issue area to another," helped to keep the diplomatic culture acting in a way which leads to (what each country saw as) "responsible" behaviour." This, he concluded, could make diplomatic relations somewhat "immune to the vagaries and personalities of the top level, its impact on the total relationship seems to be "effectively muted by the diplomatic culture."[11] It appears now that this characterization no longer reflects U.S.-Canadian relations on major questions of trade.

[11] *Ibid.*, p. 395.

OWNERSHIP OF CANADIAN INDUSTRY AND RESOURCES

Another area of public policy where acts of political calculation will be more evident than in the past is Canada's whole approach to foreign ownership of its economy. In addition to the well-documented extent of foreign (mostly U.S.) ownership of the Canadian economy discussed in part in Chapter 4, there are other dimensions of this problem that will increasingly involve government action from Ottawa and from the provincial capitals as well.

Foreign acquisitions of Canadian business, for example, have increased alarmingly in the last few years. The federal office of the Director of Investigation and Research, under the Combines Investigation Act, listed the following number of acquisitions under the jurisdiction of the Act (excluding firms whose activities do not fall within the scope of the Act): 1963 (35); 1964 (87); 1965 (74); 1966 (74); 1967 (79); 1968 (155); 1969 (102).[12] Horizontal mergers – those involving competitors selling the same products in the same market – accounted for 27 per cent of foreign takeovers, and 47 per cent of domestic mergers. Vertical mergers – acquisition of suppliers or customers – accounted for 18 per cent of the domestic and 31 per cent of the international mergers during this period.[13] Approximately 80 per cent of both domestic and international mergers occurred in the manufacturing and trade sectors of the economy.[14] The causes of foreign acquisitions can be traced to rather prosaic micro-economic realities. A study for the Economic Council of Canada examined data on mergers in Canada between 1945 and 1961 and found that the number of foreign takeovers of Canadian companies tended to rise as a function of increasing merger activity in the U.S., declining levels of corporate liquidity in Canada, and increases in business failures in Canada.[15]

It is clear as implied by the Gray Report, published in *Canadian Forum,* that other criteria such as "overall and specific contributions to the Canadian economy" will now become increasingly more important before the federal Government will allow foreign takeovers. Ottawa must concern itself with this issue not only because of the importance of the above criteria but also because although Canada's

[12] For these statistics and a list of companies see D. Godfrey, M. Watkins, eds., *Gordon to Watkins to You* (Toronto: 1970), pp. 145-161.
[13] See G. L. Reuber and F. Roseman, *The Take-Over of Canadian Firms* (Staff study for the Economic Council of Canada).
[14] *Ibid.*, p. 15.
[15] *Ibid.*

external assets (that is, Canadian investment abroad) amounted to a formidable $18.8 billion by 1967, this was only about two-fifths of gross liabilities. This left Canadians with *per capita* gross liabilities of $2,207 in 1967, compared to the comparative figure of $438 for the United States, for example (*Globe and Mail*, December 3, 1971, p. 1). *Statistics Canada* placed Canada's gross liabilities (foreign investment in Canada) at the end of 1969 at $46.9 billion (book, not market, value). A takeover review board or screening agency, under either direct or indirect political control, will generate many tough questions for any such board about the industrial strategy Canada must pursue. Ottawa must do much more work on such a strategy before the board will be able to operate with confidence. As a *Globe and Mail* editorial on December 10, 1971, put it, "How we propose to implement controls on foreign investment in Canada could be a good deal less important than the areas in which we propose to impose the controls."

The question of the industrial strategy to be promoted implicitly by this board is beginning to be faced by all three major political parties in Ottawa. All three parties now seem to emphasize the need for more processing and labour-intensive activities and it may prove difficult for many foreign buyers to succeed in their case for a takeover except on these grounds.

Yet more Canadians now also recognize that a takeover review board or screening agency even if it had a clear industrial strategy to follow, would not be greatly relevant when it comes to repatriating the economy. There remains considerable dispute about the wisdom of repatriation as an objective. The Trudeau government says it is against "buying back" the economy and its enthusiasm has centred on projects which concentrate on Canadian control of new and impending economic activity in Canada (through the CDC etc.) than on buying back the present foreign-owned industries. Insofar as it has grappled with the existing foreign economic influence in Canada, it has relied on ministerial speeches, which deal more with symbols than substance (i.e. "nationalistic" speeches by ministers and an emphasis on "territorial sovereignty" in defence policy and pollution control). The Trudeau emphasis on increasing future Canadian participation in new economic activity may reflect the lack of popular and expert agreement on the extent or nature of the economic costs of existing foreign ownership. For example, a leading Canadian student of the subject, A. E. Safarian, argues in his *The Performance of Foreign-*

Owned Firms in Canada, that the extension of U.S. law and regulations into Canada through the operations of subsidiaries is a greater danger to Canada than the proportion of Canadian industry owned by foreigners. He also argues that poor performance of firms in Canada is not related to ownership but to firm size, specialization, the effect of tariffs, and the lack of competition in the Canadian economy. Yet recent statistics show that slightly over 42 per cent of the profits of all incorporated firms are earned by foreign controlled firms. Foreign investors have clearly gone straight to the more profitable areas of the Canadian economy, and today they reap dividends which far exceed the annual inflow of U.S. investment, (see Table 7). However this unsettling piece of evidence has lead to strong disagreements in Canada. To some economists this dividend outflow should be looked upon as payment on the accumulated stock of U.S. capital in Canada, not simply on one year's flow of capital from abroad.

What continues to aggravate other Canadian observers is that the extension of American control is largely financed within Canada once the American interest has marshalled the initial capital and assumed the initial risk. Table 7 shows that retained earnings, depreciation, and depletion allowances provided approximately 66 per cent of the capital funds raised by a selected group of Canadian subsidiaries – principally for new investment and for the takeover of other Canadian companies from 1963-1965. Further, in 1968, 20.3 per cent of these funds were raised in Canadian money markets and only 4.9 per cent in American. Between 1963 and 1968 the subsidiaries surveyed (which represent a fairly good sample of all American affiliates in Canada) raised $1,244,000,000 in the United States and $2,007,000,000 in non-U.S. – mainly Canadian – money markets. It is clear then, that foreign-owned industries are absorbing substantial quantities of indigenous Canadian capital. This absorption has prompted complaints that "Canada is being bought out with its own money."

Yet to others this way of articulating the problem is deceiving since about two-thirds of capital funds are cash flows generated from retained earnings, depreciation, and depletion allowances. And if these assets are considered to be foreign-owned, then these sources must be viewed similarly. Also it is clear that foreign investment can be of substantial benefit in the long run in ways unacknowledged by its critics. Summarizing the usual argument on this latter point, one Canadian economist points to the fact that, "Over half of all the direct profit from foreign investment remains in Canada in the form of: corporation income tax payments to the Government; withholding taxes on external dividend payments; and dividends received by Canadians who directly or indirectly hold equity in foreign-controlled corporations in Canada. Additional benefits accrue to Canada through the indirect efforts of foreign investment: (1) in raising the earnings of domestic productive factors, including labour; and (2) in increasing productivity and/or reducing prices."[16]

Table 7.   Sources of New U.S. Direct Investment in Canada

Selected Years in the 1960's
($U.S. Millions)

	1963	*1964*	*1965*	*1967*	*1968*
Total Investment	1,666	2,038	2,656	2,527	2,611
Retained Earnings	675	863	852	925	1,027
Depreciation and Depletion	552	623	681	800	864
Funds from Abroad	241	307	497	423	539
Other Sources and Adjustments	29	88	75	138	53
Funds from the U.S.*	168	156	551	242	127
* Refers to Percentage of the total U.S. Investment	10.0%	7.6%	20.8%	9.6%	4.9%

Source: U.S. Department of Commerce, *Survey of Current Business*, L, No. 11, November 1970, Table 2, pp. 16-17.

These benefits are important. Nevertheless, this emphasis should not be allowed to obscure the fact that dividend payments are but one of a

[16] Prof. G. L. Reuber's letter in *The Globe and Mail*, Toronto, January 27, 1971, p. 7.

number of reasons which force multinational corporations to maintain foreign subsidiaries. For example, to the extent that a more or less assured market exists for the component or finished exports of a parent at prices that can be manipulated by the parent, this surely involves a "cost" to the host country. U.S. investors, in particular, prefer wholly-owned subsidiaries (unlike the Japanese, who are prepared to take a minority equity position), for this facilitates a strategy of taking the main profits through the parent. And the decisions on how to price products sold among subsidiaries can be made dependent on the tariffs and taxes prevailing in each country.

Yet many Canadian economists doubt the prevelance of such abuses and manipulations. For example, it may be true that with respect to some allegations of poor subsidiary export and research performance, suspicions of a number of foreign subsidiaries may be largely imaginary. Yet it is difficult to argue that the present pattern of multinational corporate activity in Canada, at the manufacturing level, does not, on occasion, open the way for a shifting of profit from Canada to the parent through high management fees, over-charging subsidiaries for goods bought from the parent or its other subsidiaries and through heavy charges for services supplied by the parent. It is also difficult to argue against the proposition that one of the sources of Canada's under-employment can, in some instances, be traced to an uncreative manufacturing sector and the purely extractive nature of some resource industries and this can be a result of some types of foreign investment. The encouragement in Canada of miniature replicas of foreign (largely U.S.) product lines can fulfill market needs profitably enough, and the subsidiary can therefore be discouraged from pursuing its own research and development in order to produce a different product, specifically Canadian, and suitable for export.

Many of these suspicions are so conjectural as to defy analysis. Yet the political mood on the subject of foreign ownership is bound to evoke policy commitments and these will be as much acts of faith as acts of analysis. And there should be no mistaking that the political mood already is more nationalist in a protective sense than was ever evident in the 1950's or early 1960's. Two years ago George Bain, Toronto *Globe and Mail* columnist, could suggest that there was "one thing that worries Canadians more than economic domination" and that this was "that someone, some time, would try to do something about it" (November 4, 1969, p. 6). He traced this to the habitual caution of most Canadians on questions of their pocketbook. By 1972 however this sentiment had become less evident. Not only is the Committee for an Independent Canada and the Waffle Group of the NDP making a greater educational impact on Canadians on these questions since 1969, but the Governments of Canada and Ontario have, by late 1971, in their policy papers on foreign investment, added their prestige and therefore symbolic expectation of action to this issue. By generating reports which outlined (if they did not document) the magnitude of the costs and distortions which may be involved in the high level of foreign investment in Canada, they made action almost essential.

Two leading scholars, in an analytical study of foreign policy decision-making, have suggested that major decisions in foreign policy are easier to make if a series of crises and controversies prepare the public for fundamental reform or action.[17] They argue that such highly charged situations almost demand a shift from the policy of *status quo* to something that would help to release the tension and deliver a new context. In 1969, 1970, and 1971 the federal government relied primarily on symbolic actions and acknowledgements on the issue of foreign investment. Much was made symbolically through an emphasis on territorial sovereignty in defence and foreign policy. "Acknowledgements" of the possible economic gravity of the issue were made by Ottawa in setting up a portfolio with the explicit purpose of studying the issue and by Ontario in its holding of a well-publicized conference on the issue. By 1972 governments in Canada will be moving to the substantive stage on this issue. It will be easier in the first stage, of course, to move to policies which simply discourage certain types of foreign investment. The tough stage will be the movement to policies which attempt to buy back part of the foreign investment nexus already in place. Americans however should realize that this movement in policy to a firmer position on economic nationalism is not prompted solely – if perhaps even in a major way – by visceral anti-Americanism. It is prompted fundamentally by a growing desire – even in Quebec – to gain more independence from the United States and a faith that less reliance on foreign-owned enterprise is necessary. This is an instinct that does not look like it will go away. Nor, it must be admitted, for any nation that wishes to exercise more than a modicum of political independence will this instinct be totally frustrated. The political restraints and imperatives of U.S. economic influence have been real. These will be introduced in the next chapter.

[17] See R. C. Snyder's and G. D. Paige's article in R. C. Snyder, H. W. Bruck, and B. Sapin, eds., *Foreign Policy Decision Making* (New York: 1962), pp. 239-248.

Chapter 7

Political Implications of the Canadian-American Relationship

The deepest dent made in Canadian public opinion about U.S. influence in Canada may have been made by President Nixon on August 15, 1971, when he slapped a 10 per cent surtax on a number of U.S. imports, at least 25 per cent of which affected Canada. Before this, the nationalist writers were probably more successful in reaching public opinion on the political, rather than economic, aspects of their case. In a Gallup Poll published in January 1971, 59 per cent of Canadians said that a growing concern over Canadian nationalism was a good thing for the country. Only 8 per cent said it was not. This mood can be traced in part to the fact that the experiences of Canadian and American societies have diverged rather radically in the last five years. Such developments as the American urban crisis, and the Vietnam War, have given Canadians the occasion to gain some sense of national attributes and national objectives that distinguish them from Americans. Many will say that these distinguishing features are not defined. Yet at least the search is a fact, and demands for sovereignty and freedom of action have unquestionably emerged.

Those Canadians who approach economic nationalism cautiously usually argue that the weakest link in the chain of nationalists' analysis of the Canadian condition is their failure to prove and document the supposed cause and effect relationship between economic dependence and political dependence. Political dependence has not been proven, they charge, except in so far that it is a self-fulfilling prophecy. In other words to assert that political dependence already exists may be so persuasive, that the will for independence may well collapse.

The continuing viability of the Canadian state is dependent on its members' faith in themselves – on their maintaining Canada as the focus of their identification, on their calling on Canada to help them achieve their own ends, on their acquiescing in the demands Canada makes on them. Canadian nationalists rightly see in every surrender of freedom of action a threat to continued independent existence. A loss of efficacy on the part of government to affect the environment, for example, might lead directly to a lessening of the popular will to maintain a separate statehood. The task confronting the analyst now is to try to marry the aspiration of independence with its actuality, by assessing how much freedom of action is possible, and how much is desirable, given other national objectives such as economic welfare and an enhanced quality of life.

Let us look at this "political dependence" somewhat surgically. Canada's economic linkages with the United States might restrict the freedom of government action in at least six important ways: 1) the potential threat of generalized retaliation against undesired Canadian behaviour; 2) the threat of specific retaliation for actions of economic policy detrimental to American interests; 3) the inability to affect business policies because of the transfer of decision-making to the United States; 4) the extra-territorial application of American laws and regulations in Canada; 5) the "penetrative influences" of American multinational corporations as carriers of American cultural values and political influences promoting American objectives; and 6) involvement by implication (for example, defence production sharing agreements).

THE THREAT OF GENERALIZED RETALIATION

One hypothesis which has figured prominently in the current debate on Canadian independence is the likelihood of retaliation by the United States government along the whole front of economic linkages[1]

[1] See P. V. Lyon, *The Policy Question* (Toronto: McClelland and Stewart, 1963), p. 27, "I know of only one occasion when the Americans may have coupled a political issue to a Canadian request for consideration in a trade matter. This was a statement by Dulles which appeared to be a threat to reduce the quota on oil imports from Canada if we refused to change our position on the expansion of membership of the U.N."

as a consequence of undesired behaviour by Canada. This generalized threat of retaliation for acts of *political* independence can be distinguished from the threat of specific retaliation against acts of Canadian *economic* policy, in which case the primary objectives of both sides are presumably the achievement of some economic benefit or the avoidance of some economic cost. The generalized threat of economic retaliation is more directly an impingement on Canada's freedom of action in international affairs. It has, for example, often been cited as the cause of Canada's non-recognition of China for twenty-one years.

There is very little public evidence of this kind of retaliation or of actual threat. Clearly it would require a detailed knowledge of the origins of certain American policies to be able to know for sure. It is a fact, however, that economic dependence has not prevented Canada from public disagreement with the United States on numerous occasions. In discussing Canadian independence, many Americans concentrate on Canada's diplomatic posture more than its economic dependence on the U.S. as a basis for their perceptions. For example, one correspondent for the *Chicago Tribune*, wrote that he could not see any evidence for the "dependence" argument in Canadian actions in 1971. Expressing astonishment at the inclination of Canadians to view their country as a "mouse" compared to the U.S. "elephant," he wrote that this:

> ... must be an irony for the White House and the State Department.

> Since World War II, Canada has almost always gone its own way rather than follow American policy, as in the cases of Cuba, Communist China, and Viet Nam.

> Mitchell Sharp, Secretary of State for External Affairs, speaks of the U.S. as Canada's "closest friend and ally" in dinner speeches. However, in stating policy on the floor of the House of Commons, he upholds the Canadian post-war tradition of being America's severest critic.

> "Canada has taken the lead of all countries in protesting the Amchitka test," Sharp said to applause in Commons. He also said that Canada, after Albania, had taken the lead in getting Communist China admitted to the United Nations at the cost of the expulsion of Taiwan over American objections.

Canadian complaints and protest about American policy provide material for Communist Chinese and Soviet correspondents here, who seek anti-American stories. Peking's correspondent writes almost exclusively about alleged mistreatment of Canada by the U.S., according to what has been seen of his dispatches.[2]

But even in the absence of its demonstration, the potential of economic retaliation has helped determine the parameters of Canadian freedom of action. Former Prime Minister Lester Pearson has explicitly referred to this potential as a factor in his own thinking about Canadian independence.[3] Canadian governments have probably believed themselves to be possessed of a lesser degree of freedom of action on its account.

What makes this a plausible hypothesis is that many of the economic linkages between Canada and the United States are the result of special bilateral arrangements. While these arrangements serve American interests, the initiative for each has more often come from Canada, and one of the chief jobs of Canadian negotiators has been to argue the benefits for the United States. The need for a special arrangement has appeared higher on the Canadian list of priorities than on the American. And it therefore seems to follow that Canadian negotiators worry more about preserving an atmosphere of good will in relations with the United States, than vice-versa.

It is noticeable that the tendency of the Trudeau Government is to put somewhat less emphasis on ambiance and "good will" on a number of issues. The abruptness of the announced intention to establish a 12-mile territorial sea limit, pollution control zones, and fisheries closing lines, is clear evidence of that.[4] In part, the Canadian Government may now be more sceptical of the efficacy of strategies which are based solely on the gamble that "good will" will prevail and

[2] November 22, 1971, p. 10.

[3] "We can't ignore the fact that the first result of any open breach with the United States over Vietnam, which their government considered to be unfair and unfriendly on our part, would be a more critical examination by Washington of certain aspects of our relationship from which we, as well as they, get great benefit."–quoted in Kari Levitt, *Silent Surrender* (Toronto: Macmillan, 1970), p. 2.

[4] This action also reflects the fact that the *functional* departments, for example the Department of Fisheries, are enjoying a greater say in policy towards the U.S. than the Department of External Affairs, which is occupationally concerned with ambience, and which undoubtedly considered the government's arctic and fisheries policies unnecessary and provocative.

will lead to mutual adjustments. It must also be calculating that it has sufficient bargaining advantages of its own at the moment to deal with Washington on an arm's length basis, notably in the resource area.

THE THREAT OF SPECIFIC RETALIATION

There is much more evidence for what might be termed the threat of specific retaliation, that is American economic reprisals against what are perceived as hostile acts of Canadian economic policy. This threat is really just a logical concomitant of the reciprocal nature of economic relationships in an interdependent world. Retaliation may be an arbitrary act of policy, as when the U.S. Administration threatened retaliation against the American agencies of Canadian banks after the decennial revision of Canada's Bank Act curbed the growth of First National City Bank's Canadian subsidiary. Or it may be automatic, as when the Modene Radiator Company of Racine, Wisconsin, brought a complaint to the U.S. Customs Bureau against the Canadian "duty remission plan" which accorded the equivalent of an export subsidy to Canada's automotive industry. In the event, neither threat worked: in the first case Canada called the American bluff; in the second, the Auto Pact was introduced to break a potential spiral of retaliation.

A more important example was the threat posed to Canada by the prospect of being cut off from U.S. capital markets, as signified by the run on Canadian foreign exchange reserves in both 1963 and 1968 when restrictive measures were instituted in Washington. In the former case, a Canadian delegation immediately flew to Washington and achieved an exemption for Canada, but at the cost of a Canadian commitment to maintain its gold and dollar reserves at the level of $2.6 billion. The commitment served as a significant impingement on Canadian control of its monetary policy during the middle sixties. In order that the limit on reserves not be exceeded, it appeared that Canada could not permit interest rates to become more attractive than American rates. This disability undoubtedly hampered Canadian efforts to curb the inflationary situation that had grown very serious by the latter part of the decade.

This evident narrowing of Canada's policy options did not arouse much complaint at the time and many people on both sides of the border would probably consider it an acceptable price for benefits received. They might, with justification, argue that the essential meaning of *independence* is the facility to determine modes of *interdepend-*

ence. Accepting the fact of United States economic preponderance as a virtual constant in Canadian policy-making, the advocates of interdependence might go on to defend the merits of an explicit strategy of specialization for the Canadian economy, so as to maximize the benefits of efficiency throughout the continent.

The "interdependence argument" simply emphasizes how subtle but serious a threat is posed to Canada's political sovereignty by the preponderant weight of American economic power. For in the national pursuit of economic ends Canada may put herself in such a position of dependence that the credibility of her political instruments is later compromised. A government that is prevented from applying the full range of policies at its disposal to fight inflation for example, may be fulfilling its external obligations, but not its obligations to its own constituency. These latter obligations are more directly related to the social objectives that are debated in Canada today and, therefore, Canadians will consider their fulfillment to be the more crucial exercise, indeed the litmus test, of sovereignty.

THE INABILITY TO AFFECT BUSINESS POLICIES

The transfer of business decision-making from the country represents another significant restraint on the freedom of action of Canadian governments. Government is now thoroughly accustomed to trying to achieve public policy goals – in the areas of employment, the cost of living, aggregate demand, and export trade – through influencing private enterprise decisions by means of a host of measures that range from moral persuasion to physical controls. If the companies within its jurisdiction are impotent, then government will be likewise impotent. An example of this emerged in March of 1968, when the Canadian Minister of Finance had to intercede with the U.S. Secretary of the Treasury in order to stop Canadian subsidiaries from returning funds to the U.S. in response to compulsory guidelines.

An integration of markets can simply concentrate the trend towards integration of business policy-making, and its transference from the "hinterland" to the "metropolis." The 1965 auto agreement undoubtedly has brought Canada considerable balance-of-payments benefits and probably some employment benefits (though these are at the lower-skilled end of the scale, as an almost complete concentration of engineering and design personnel has occurred in the American headquarters). It has, however, led to virtually complete centralization of manufacturing and purchasing decisions in the American head offices. At Ford of Canada, for example, which was the most autonomous of the "Big Three" Canadian subsidiaries, the management of its overseas operations has now been transferred to the International Division of the U.S. Company, and personnel responsible for manufacturing decisions are directly under the command of the North American Sales Division.

Canadian analysts have distinguished between the executive functions of the corporations' head office – formulation of long-range goals, decisions on investment, exports, product development, and allocation of basic tasks – from the managerial functions of specific price, marketing, and personnel decisions performed by the subsidiary. It is hypothesized that the subsidiary is regarded by the parent, not as a separate corporate entity, but as one element in an overall pattern of production and sales; that it is valued for exploiting some particular advantage in its own area in the service of an overall corporate strategy, rather than necessarily rendering a profit for itself. A devaluation of the currency, for example, would not affect trade between the subsidiaries of a parent company that can dictate the prices of goods moving between them. Much of this analysis is so plausible in some instances and so implausible in others, that it deserves immediate and careful research.

Early research has revealed that capital expenditures are the items most carefully controlled by the parent, with product innovation second. Much more research is needed on various hypotheses on the impact of multinational corporations, but no amount of research, of course, will qualify the fact of ultimate control vested in the parent.

EXTRATERRITORIALITY

The extraterritorial application of American laws and regulations to Canadian subsidiaries is unanimously recognized as an abuse of Canadian sovereignty. This problem is an unnecessary irritant in relations between the two countries. A 1971 Presidential Commission has already urged that the application of American law on American subsidiaries be eased. There is a danger, however, that Canadian concentration on the problem of extraterritoriality might become a substitute for an overall policy on foreign ownership. The extraterritorial application of U.S. laws qualifies Canadian jurisdiction over resident corporations, and reduces the capacity of Canadian governments to implement distinctive economic policies. A number of U.S. laws and regulations prohibit trade with communist countries, for example, and carry penalties for the officers of parent firms that permit their foreign subsidiaries to conduct such trade. This is the most notorious abuse because it reflects a foreign policy position quite inconsistent with that taken by Canada. More significant are the efforts of the U.S. Government and courts to enforce American anti-trust laws on Canadian subsidiaries.

There are many known instances of this, and significant sectors of the Canadian economy have undoubtedly felt the impact of an imposed view of business competition that is appropriate to the American, not the Canadian, context. Finally, there is the extraterritorial application of balance of payments regulations, such as the voluntary guidelines of 1966, which were made mandatory in 1968, and from which Canada eventually secured an exemption in large part. Especially galling to Canadians was the principle that U.S. regulations could force Canadian subsidiaries to declare dividends to their American parents whether or not it was in their interests as Canadian companies.

Canada and the United States have reached a number of agreements on the question of extraterritoriality, providing for consultation on specific cases as they arise, and they do signify the desire of both countries to remove this cause of abrasiveness between them. As a result of the Eisenhower-Diefenbaker agreement of 1958, some exemptions have been granted by the U.S. Government with respect to the Foreign Assets Control Regulations which were affecting Canadian exports. Recently, the regulations were relaxed to permit all foreign subsidiaries to trade with China, through permission is still to be granted on a case-by-case basis, and the American component of the export item must, in general, be non-strategic in nature and less than 50 per cent of the item's value. The Fulton-Rogers, and later, the Basford-Mitchell agreements have likewise eased the situation with respect to the extraterritorial application of U.S. anti-trust law.

Yet there remains a strong suspicion on the part of interested Canadians that corporate decisions of subsidiaries are still very much influenced by the importance attached by their head offices of maintaining good relations with Washington. Few documented instances seem to exist of Canadian subsidiaries foregoing orders from communist countries. But neither is it likely that these subsidiaries have been mounting aggressive drives to capture export markets in such countries. The establishment of diplomatic relations between Canada and China has made possible much broader trade relations between the two countries, and any unwillingness on the part of American-controlled companies to participate in these relations will be more noticeable and even more irksome to Canadians than before.

Two different approaches to this problem of extraterritoriality have emerged from Ottawa, and they reflect fairly deep differences on the whole subject of Canada's relations with the United States. On the one hand, some insist that the *ad hoc* methods are working fairly well; that in most cases the problem is simply one of correcting American oversight, and that if Canadian subsidiaries are informally influenced by American laws, then so are Canadian-owned and controlled companies which do a large part of their business in the United States. This is an application of the doctrine of inter-dependence: a flexible attitude to the inconveniences and excesses occasioned by an insensitive and powerful nation, coupled with a forthright defence of specific, tangible, economic interests. It is an approach perhaps best typified by the Pearson Government's relations with the United States.

Opposed to that outlook is the doctrine that emphasizes that relations between states are *sui generis* and not to be confused by analogy with relations between persons or private interests. The predominance of that analogy is, in fact, the real danger that emerges from a relationship as sustained and intimate as that between Canada and the United States. It is the *principle* of non-interference by American legislation or regulation that matters, rather than individual instances of it. The current arrangements to deal with extraterritoriality are unsatisfactory for being *ad hoc*, and for failing to counteract unseen but powerful influences of U.S. policy on Canadian companies. Therefore, a government export agency (recommended first in the Watkins Report on foreign ownership), may be necessary to act as an intermediary between U.S. subsidiaries and markets to which their exports are prohibited by law. A Parliamentary Committee even offered some cautious support to a suggestion that the federal government should appoint a trustee to exercise the voting rights of foreign-owned shares of corporations affected by extraterritorial laws during the time of the application of those laws.[5]

It must not be forgotten that this strategy of explicit, institutionalized reprisal would horrify the large group of Canadians who are accustomed to pragmatic, business-like dealings with Americans. The consequence of such remedies might be a highly visible preservation

---

[5] *Report on Canada-U.S. Relations*, House of Commons Standing Committee on External Affairs and National Defence, Proceedings, 1970, No. 33.

of sovereignty at the cost of a considerable increase in continental acrimony. Yet a significant number of Canadians are now prepared to say that the disease is worse than the remedy.

PENETRATIVE INFLUENCES

Although adequate research on the subject is lacking on the possible penetrative activities of American economic power, the ways in which its agents manage to act from *within* the Canadian political system, rather than from outside (where they are clearly recognizable as external influences), has become a cause of concern to Canadians. "Penetration" should not, however, have a uniformly pejorative meaning. Nor is it completely one-way. Canadians should acknowledge that their interests have successfully penetrated the American system, by way of the American multinational corporation. Big oil companies with large Canadian interests, like Continental and Gulf, made submissions on behalf of an open market for Canadian oil imports before a Presidential Task Force. At least two of the "Big Three" auto companies lobbied for the Auto Pact. And a California Congressman, whose district contains a large part of the Douglas Aircraft Company, re-introduced a bill in 1970, highly favourable to Canada, which would enable reductions in the U.S. tariff on Canadian goods, in particular aircraft parts imported by Douglas.[6]

Virtually nothing is known publicly about the lobbying activities in Ottawa of American subsidiaries. Nevertheless theorists of multinational corporations hold that such corporations have an interest in enhancing the predictability and uniformity of the environments within which they operate, and that amicable and steady relations between the various national segments of that environment are needed. It is also believed that foreign corporations are carriers of the cultural values of their country of origin, or, more generally, of the values of a liberal ideology of technological progress, which they propagate by means of such demand-creating mechanisms as product differentiation and advertising. Some nationalist philosophers in Canada fear that the prime threat to Canadian independence is the homogenizing influence of this ideology, of which the United States, by virtue of its technological leadership, is the chief bearer. John Kenneth Galbraith, for example, has argued that the stultifying impact of a burgeoning technostructure cannot be clearly differentiated from the intrusion of American policy, so

[6] H. R. 3263, 92d Congress, 1st session, introduced by Representative James C. Corman (Dem., Calif.).

that the rebellion against the phenomenon of technology, when pitched on universal principles, becomes fuel for nationalist resentment of American domination. Galbraith insists however that Canadians should make the distinction between U.S. policy and technological threats to culture (see *Toronto Star*, October 23, 1971, p. 1).

Of major importance to Canadians is the impact of foreign ownership on domestic integration. One of the most serious charges is that U.S. direct investment has had a regionally disintegrative effect in so far as it has captured the allegiance of an Anglo-Saxon business élite, concentrated in central Canada; strengthened its position *vis-à-vis* the rest of the country and other strata of society; and constructed permanent links between that élite and the fountainhead of wealth and power in the United States. This process of disintegration has, the thesis claims, been helped by the Canadian federal structure which gives power over resource development to the provincial governments, all of which avidly pursue the goal of maximum economic development in the quickest possible time.

Finally, it should be recognized that a type of "international interest group" structure has been set up through multinational corporations. This structure has a tendency to promote what Harvard political scientist, Karl Deutsch, has called a "pluralist security community," which is a "relationship of separate states where problems are solved by peaceful change." This structure is also a form of penetration, and is expected to promote a general feeling of community among North Atlantic countries as powerful in the 1970's as any military alliance in the 1940's and 1950's. Another American observer's description has obvious implications for Canada:

> . . . the three essential conditions for a pluralistic security community are 1) compatibility of major values relevant to political decision-making; 2) capacity of participating political units to respond peacefully to each other's needs and communications; and 3) mutual predictability of behavior. Multinational firms, insofar as they are political actors, i.e., insofar as they are not only devoted to profit-seeking in a free market situation but are also devoted to security and autonomy through controlling and superseding the market, have, in certain situations, helped to create these essential conditions. They seek to transfer values on such matters as management behavior, technological growth, and consumer behavior between countries. These values can reinforce peaceful behavior

and mutual predictability because multinational enterprises require increasing economic interdependence. For example, they work for such developments as European patent systems and a common currency. In addition, it is well known that most international communications in the world take the form of commercial messages.[7]

When Ontario Premier John Robarts once said that U.S. investment in his province was a "phony issue" or that it had "never been a real concern," he may have been expressing how these values unconsciously affected him.

Yet the homogenization of western society through such penetrative influences can be vastly exaggerated. To begin with, it does not necessarily carry over fully into foreign policy. Canadian consciousness of how American foreign policy can diverge from that of Canada is unmistakable. The only question is how fervent the consciousness is. Canadians may not share the language of one Canadian commentator, speaking to an American audience in 1971, but there is little doubt that they agree with the conclusion:

> It was still possible to recite, with some reasonable show of conviction, what an analyst of Canadian-American relations stated fifteen years [ago] "One thing is fundamental at the outset. The two countries share an identity of basic aims – an identity so complete that it is normally taken for granted in any discussion of their relations." Today that is no longer true.

> It is no longer true in North America. The main strategic threat to Canada comes not from our north but from our south. The Pax Americana once reached all around the world. Now it's being driven back upon a continental base. But "empire" is as American as cherry pie. As the imperial perimeter contracts – in Southeast Asia, in Latin America, even in Western Europe – the hard-driving entrepreneurs who have made this country what it is today are opening up a new empire in their own backyard. Canada is serving as a decompression chamber for a new generation of American imperialists during their transition to another level and venue of domination.

[7] Jonathon Galloway "The Multinational Corporation As An International Interest Group." A Paper presented to the American Political Science Association, Los Angeles, California, September, 1970.

It is not the sort of manifest destiny I desire for my country, any more than you would desire it for your own.[8]

INVOLVEMENT BY IMPLICATION

Since the Hyde Park Declaration of 1941, Canada has concluded about twelve declarations and agreements with the United States that have as their purpose the cooperation of the two countries in meeting each other's defence needs. In particular, the cancellation of the prestigious but prohibitively expensive CF-105 Arrow aircraft program in 1959 made it traumatically evident to the Canadian Government that the country could not produce major items of defence equipment for Canadian consumption alone. It was determined that, if a defence industry were to be preserved at all, Canada's best course was to develop specialized equipment, often related to her indigenous needs, such as transport and communication equipment. Canada would then attempt to gain access for these to the much greater American market for defence goods. The agreements were never intended to operate in a perfectly reciprocal fashion. Essentially, the United States gave Canada privileged access to her market because Canada was a good ally and was dependent on the U.S. for 50 to 60 per cent of her defence supplies. Later on, the U.S. Government became concerned about the balance of payments effects and a rough reciprocity of purchases was agreed upon. At present, purchases are weighted in Canada's favour because of America's needs for the Vietnam War.

Under the agreements, Canadian industry is, in general, permitted to compete with United States industry for United States defence contracts. The United States Government has waived the "Buy American" Act for most Canadian defence items and remitted customs duties on a very wide range of such items. In the decade after 1959, the United States purchased $508 million more defence items[9] in Canada than Canada purchased in the United States. Over 150 Canadian companies participate in these export sales at the present time. The program has thus been of benefit to the Canadian balance of payments, to employment in Canada, and to the technological efficiency of Canadian industry, as well as in meeting Canada's defence commitments. The antipathy to the defence agreements exhibited by such ar-

[8] Prof. James Eayrs of the University of Toronto speaking to the 12th Annual Seminar on Canadian-United States Relations, Columbia University, New York, November 17, 1970.

[9] The *Financial Post*, October 30, 1971, pp. 1, 2.

ticulate and thoughtful organs of Canadian public opinion as *Maclean's Magazine*, and the *Toronto Star*, is balanced by the federal government's concern about the possibly adverse reaction of mining locals in Sudbury, and aircraft workers in Montreal and Toronto, to the results of the abrogation of these agreements. It must be remembered, however, that many companies producing defence items in Canada are, in fact, U.S. owned, and therefore the U.S. benefits through dividends and through other means.

Clearly the defence production agreements are of such sensitive nature that they could only have been concluded by nations sharing a rough identity of aims and attitudes. It is likewise clear that the United States would at once cease her dependence on Canada for some selected lines of military equipment if Canada took radically divergent positions in international affairs that clearly implied the absence of this fundamental identity of view and purpose. It is this point which lends potency to the critics' argument that the agreements imply Canadian approval of American foreign policy, particularly in Vietnam. A Canadian decision to abrogate the agreements could do nothing to affect American actions in Vietnam, but the agreements may be a factor in what is termed the "blurred image" of Canada abroad.

One critic told the Parliamentary Committee on External Affairs and National Defence, that the major objectives of Canadian foreign policy should be "the creation of a distinct image in the external world of an autonomous Canadian identity as an actor in the international community."[10] The Trudeau White Paper explicitly rejected this approach. It seemed to question the fact that a nation's image can be affected by individual policy acts, or that such an image is a viable goal of policy at all. Moreover, the argument that the production sharing agreements represent an impingement on Canada's independence is most effectively made if it can be shown that her international image is a distortion of that which Canadians desire to project. This the critics have as yet failed to do. Still, times are changing. In the early 1960's it could be realistically argued that complete non-alignment was intellectually possible, but socially and politically impossible, since Canadians were not neutral people. In the 1970's, because of the Vietnam War and U.S.-Canadian differences, this gap may be narrower.

[10] Professor Michael Brecher, see, *Minutes of Proceedings and Evidence of the House of Commons Standing Committee on External Affairs and National Defence*, February 13, 1969, p. 952.

In the peculiarly introspective mood of Canada today, "international image" is often a cover for "self-image," and most criticisms against the defence agreements are essentially from a moral viewpoint, the desire not to be involved, whatever the cost, and whatever the practical insignificance of the act. That is an aim less to be argued than to be analyzed, as an instance of the heavy psychic demands placed on contemporary political systems and the peculiarly amorphous contours that the concept of "political responsibility" has acquired in our time.

CONCLUSION

Would a determinedly "independent" Canada embark on a road to inevitable frustration? In its less palatable version, the argument of interdependence is a forthright statement of the inevitability of *dependence*. Judd Polk, in a paper prepared for a Columbia University conference on Canadian-American relations in 1970, argued that the most significant continental linkages simply are not susceptible to national treatment on Canada's part. The Canadian tax structure cannot diverge too radically from the American; wage pressures in the more advanced industrial economy are bound to be communicated north of the border, and so on. Even by itself, the catalogue of linkages appears to make an overwhelming case for continued interdependence: the paper estimates that 54 per cent of Canada's GNP is the product of American investment and imports; financial and money markets are one; financial institutions are intermeshed; foreign ownership and most of its effects are facts of life; to consider breaking the links is to think the unthinkable.

This is an argument more noteworthy for its psychological than its intellectual power. But it suggests very strongly that the economic relationship does yield definite parameters that have governed Canadian freedom of action; that there is an immovable *structure* concealed beneath the mass of day-to-day dealings between Canada and the United States. The great dilemma confronting Canada now is that these parameters have never been tested much before 1971 owing to the previously mentioned shared attitudes and objectives. This no doubt helps to account for the great distance between the ambitious advocacy of Canadian autonomy on one side of the current debate, and the sober acceptance of interdependence on the other.

Chapter 8

Other Dimensions of Canadian Foreign Policy: The Decline of Voluntarism beyond North America

FROM 1945 TO 1975

It would be easy to forget, in the emphasis on Canada's international economic problems in the previous chapters, that Canadian foreign policy, especially since World War II, has exhibited an "internationalist" thrust, at times it has appeared to be almost an altruistic thrust. The internationalist emphasis in most cases, has not been difficult to square with Canadian national interests. Canada's interest in world trade liberalization is complemented by a Canadian emphasis on internationalism. Canada's impotence to affect through its own power any world military configuration has made it useful for it to support NATO and NORAD where at least formal consultation with allies is provided. Canada's search for both material and symbolic counterweights to the United States has lead to a Canadian cultivation of European contacts, vigorous efforts to hold the Commonwealth together and relentless efforts to help prop up and sustain the United Nations. Canada's helplessness – unilaterally – to materially diminish the arms race has always channeled considerable Canadian enthusiasm, patience and rhetoric behind any east-west disarmament or mutual security agreements. Also Canadian fears that small crises can escalate to major power confrontations have lead to a Canadian willingness to contribute to UN-sponsored peace-keeping ventures and to steadfast if monotonous Canadian requests to the belligerents "to come to the conference table to settle differences peaceably." Clearly then, "internationalism" in most cases has been powered naturally by Canadian "national interests."

Until recently, another characteristic besides "internationalism" has been present in Canadian external policy.

Canada's post-war defence contributions to NATO and to peace-keeping can be understood in part as expressions of a trait unique to Anglo-American experience – the "voluntarist" impulse, (the emphasis in policy statements, concerning distant international constellations, on acts of faith and good will and a de-emphasis on empirical restraints). Geographical, and to some extent historical, separation from the European continent helped at one time to contribute to a "voluntarist" outlook on world affairs in the Anglo-American tradition. The tradition of national rivalries, suspicion, and hostility in Europe, have appeared to the U.S., Canada and Britain to have made only national survival the goal of European diplomatic activity. Yet Canadians, Americans, and to some extent the British, watching this scene from afar, have been impatient with, and somewhat uncomprehending of continental Europe's Hobbesian stratagems, selfishness, and conflict. In the past, voluntarist Canadians and Americans have been more attracted by the opportunities to forge "new" principles into international relations, to try to elevate the whole nature of these relations above the unsavoury business of balance-of-power politics.[1]

"It was European policy, European statesmanship, European ambition that drenched this world with blood," complained the Canadian delegate to the First Assembly of the League of Nations. Prime Minister Arthur Meighen congratulated his delegate for stating so frankly "the price the world has paid for European diplomacy of the last hundred years."[2] This attitude so shaped Canada's view of Europe that it was both continued and transformed when Canada played an active, even an initiating, role in the creation of the North Atlantic Treaty Organization from late 1947 to March, 1949. Superficially this sudden and self-willed immersion in European balance-of-power politics might appear as the end of the voluntarist syndrome in Canadian foreign policy. In fact, the Canadian attitude to the alliance was even more voluntarist than that of the United States. Canada appeared, during the preliminary negotiation of the treaty, as if it were the only nation anxious to concentrate on the *ought* of a better world order, instead of relying solely on the existing unhappy conditions of power balance in Europe. In accord with this, the Canadian government invented and worked steadfastly for the inclusion of Article 2 into the treaty organization's Charter. This Article, commonly called the "Canadian Article," expressed the intentions of the signato-

[1] See Arnold Wolfers and Lawrence Martin, eds., *The Anglo-American Tradition in Foreign Affairs* (New Haven: 1956).
[2] James Eayrs, *In Defence of Canada* (Toronto: 1964), Vol. 1, p. 3.

ry nations to develop relations not only in the military, but in economic and cultural fields as well. (Canada's heavy participation in peacekeeping ventures and unstinting effort in disarmament negotiations since the early 1950's have flowed, in part, from this voluntarist outlook as well.)

By 1960, however, the world did not seem to be accommodating itself to anyone's projects of voluntarism, let alone Canada's. Progress through peacekeeping, the UN, NATO, and disarmament negotiations, was imperceptible, if not non-existent. As early as 1963, John Holmes, Director General of the Canadian Institute of Internal Affairs, could write of the need for Canada to search for a function in the world in order to allow Canada "to feel responsible, to fulfill a mission, limited though this may be."[3] Another observer, reviewing the Diefenbaker years and the prospects for the 1960's under a Liberal Government, called for a clear identification of Canada's role in the world.[4] True voluntarism in the international system was hampered by rigidities and lack of manoeuvrability, and this resulted in massive introspection in Canada.

Voluntarism was not jettisoned by Canada in the 1960's, but the impulse was re-directed in most instances into a more limited context. It was redirected in a way that was able to command a modicum of domestic support: it emphasized Canada's role and influence in holding "international" organizations together (the UN, NATO, the Commonwealth), as well as emphasizing Canadian contributions to international police actions, and calls for belligerents to come to the conference table. It may not be far fetched to describe this as Canada's "federalist" approach to world politics, because the "organization-maintenance" and brokerage tactics the Pearson Government found essential within Canada from 1963-1968 could be comprehensibly transposed to the international system.[5] This tendency to put organizational viability before purposes of organizations, to present ambiguous schemes for peacekeeping, and to put insistent emphasis on the curative powers of negotiating tables began to be attacked by spokesmen in all major political parties by 1967 however. By the time the decision was to be made on NATO in April 1969 by the new Trudeau

[3] John Holmes "Canada In Search of Its Role," *Foreign Affairs*, July, 1963, p. 663.
[4] Peyton Lyon, *The Policy Question* (Toronto: 1960).
[5] This interpretation of the Pearson years is developed at length in T. Hockin, "The Federalist Style In Canadian Foreign Policy," in S. Clarkson, ed., *An Independent Foreign Policy for Canada*? (Toronto: 1968).

Government it was clear that the Atlantic Alliance had proved to be an expensive and profitless arena for the proponents of voluntarist action. Also the "organization-maintenance" arguments for heavy Canadian contributions to NATO were wearing thin as well because Canada's influence in the alliance was either chimerical or if real, could be destroyed if Canada boasted of it in public.[6] All this experience in the military arena combined nicely with the new emphasis of the Trudeau Government which has dismissed the "helpful fixer" role of the 1950's and 1960's as inadequate as a basis for policy on its own terms, and useful only if it can be clearly linked to national interests. As a result, the Trudeau Government found Canada's NATO commitments too expensive in terms of the country's other national interests in foreign policy, and Canada's military contribution to NATO was halved.

THE CHANGING NATURE OF CANADIAN DEFENCE POLICY

It now appears that the emphasis on voluntarist action has contracted and Canada has become more like the old Europeans in their emphasis on protection of national sovereignty and integrity. This shift can be most clearly seen in the Trudeau Government's idea of the "continental defence of North America." In fact, there is something false in organizing a description of Canada's North American military activity as an exercise in continental defence. It is to phrase it in a way more atuned to the perceptions of Canadians in the 1950's than the 1970's. A majority of Canadians may now be as worried about defence of their territorial sovereignty against Americans as about military defences against Russians or Chinese. In all three major federal political parties, the rise of anti-continentalist movements, and the concern for pollution controls, sovereignty, and fishing rights combine to put a whole new perspective on the old meaning of the "defence of North America." In fact the 1971 White Paper on Defence ranks "the defence of North America in cooperation with U.S. forces" as a second priority. The first priority is "the surveillance of our own territory and coastlines, that is, the protection of our sovereignty."

This de-emphasis of joint U.S.-Canadian activities, in NORAD in particular, cannot be viewed as a major shock to the Americans. Canada and the United States have co-operated through NORAD since

---

[6] See L. Hertzman, J. Warnock, T. Hockin, *Alliances And Illusions* (Edmonton: 1969), Part III.

1957 and in the bomber defence of North America, yet the U.S., each year, has always spent more than ten times Canada's contribution to NORAD. For example, the U.S. spent about $1.7 billion on NORAD in 1968-69, and employed 160,000 men in activities connected with continental air defence. Canada spent $167,384,000 in 1969-70, and assigned approximately 14,000 man-years to specific NORAD tasks in Canada and the U.S.[7] Canadian forces committed in past years to the air defence of North America are: 2 squadrons of Bomarc B anti-aircraft missiles equipped with nuclear war heads, 3 squadrons (48 aircraft) of nuclear-equipped CF-101 Voodoos, and improved F-101's from the U.S. Air Force. The Defence White Paper indicates that these will be phased out and replaced by updated aircraft to be employed in second-strike, defence, and deterrent roles. Although Canada's contribution may not appear to be large, it would be difficult to expect a greater quantitative contribution, since the decision-making structure on the strategy and tactics of the air defence of North America is not exactly a Canadian preserve – U.S. paramountcy is everywhere apparent.

Since the NORAD renewal, in March 1968, Canada has had to consider all dimensions of U.S.-Canadian relations, and this has had implications for defence. Also conflicts over sovereignty in the Arctic, aggravated since the voyage of the *Manhattan*, together with economic disputes, suggest that any renewal of the NORAD agreement in 1973 will cause controversy in Canada. Any federal government proposal to allow U.S. ABM bases or increased NORAD facilities in Canada could threaten the life of a Canadian government supporting either. Instead, as the Defence White Paper makes clear, Canadian military activity will concentrate increasingly on voluntarist tasks within Canada designed to protect and affirm Canadian sovereignty. Canada, in the words of one shrewd defence analyst, is moving from an alliance-oriented defence policy, to an independent defence policy, which provides a framework in which "we would offer to our allies what we had instead of providing ourselves with what they wanted." (John Gellner in the *Commentator*, September, 1971, p. 22.)

It is possible for the first time, therefore, to see here the beginnings of a "strategy" for Canadian military activity. As such, however, it calls for a redefinition of the role of the Canadian armed forces. The deployment of forces is now as closely tied to domestic non-military activity as

[7] Government of Canada, *Estimates for the Fiscal Year Ending March 31, 1972* (Ottawa: 1971), p. 15-14.

it is to specifically military assignments. Since 1968 Canadian Defence Ministers have envisaged an active role for Canada for both long-range surveillance aircraft in the north, and for adequate submarine capability for research and control over the Canadian seabed. The Canadian government is therefore faced with a major equipment decision to provide what is called a "long-range aircraft of substantial size, with a capacity to operate electronic systems" in order to exercise surveillance. This activity would not be confined simply to "looking for hostile submarines, but exercising surveillance over foreign fishing fleets which may be invading Canadian territorial waters, exercising surveillance of possible attempts to exploit the continental shelf without our permission, and possible incursions by land and by sea in our territory in the north."[8] Judging by the way in which these equipment problems are phrased it appears that there will be a mixture of civilian, as well as military "objectives" commanding decisions on equipment.

This shift appears to be in line with missions envisaged for other maritime forces as well. For example, the House Subcommittee on Maritime Forces recommended, as the *Globe and Mail* noted, June 27, 1970, that Canada's maritime forces "should play a more limited role in North Atlantic strategy, sharply scale down their concentration on anti-submarine warfare, and place priority on maintaining Canadian sovereignty, particularly in the Arctic." In the final drafting stages of the Committee report, advocates of a larger Canadian input into North Atlantic defence lost ground to those arguing that maritime forces ought to become, in effect, a super Coast-Guard service. The report's conclusion leaned heavily in this second direction. It points out that anti-submarine warfare (ASW) has changed radically: first, when the submarine changed from being a commerce raider to a missile-carrying craft, and secondly, when the Soviet Union developed nuclear-powered submarines with a missile range of 1,500 miles. It suggests that land-based, anti-ballistic missile defences will take over part of the ASW role, while the continental shelf will be policed by other means. These changes, it says, have "rendered obsolete to a large extent the concept of a self-contained ASW force at sea." The arguments which proved most persuasive to the Liberals on this key committee, which discussed proposals for nuclear-powered submarines (if the price is right), were not those advocating anti-submarine "hunter-kill" roles, but those for submarines capable of year-round operation in Arctic waters for "subsurface surveillance"; submarines to help chart underwater pinnacles along possible submarine transport routes; and submarines that can help develop technology if Arctic oil is ever to be transported by submarine tanker. For Arctic surveillance, it urged the acquisition, if economically and technically feasible, of a "subsurface perimeter surveillance system to cover the entrance to channels." The subcommittee (the *Globe* notes) discounted ideas "that Canadian forces have any future role in protection convoys to supply Europe in any emergency, or in joining NATO allies in a nuclear war at sea. The reason given was simple: there won't be a need for convoys because there won't be such a war." Instead, the committee recommended the construction of fast, light surface vessels for the role of coastal protection. The 1971 White Paper on Defence appears to have agreed with these conclusions.

INTERNATIONALISM WITHOUT VOLUNTARISM IN FOREIGN POLICY

Events of the late sixties and early seventies may also point to a similar perceptible shift in the character and motive of Canadian external policy in questions other then defence. This shift may have been both obscured and exaggerated however by some critics who have portrayed it as a movement away from an "internationalist" emphasis to isolationism. In fact the Trudeau government, if anything, has broadened the geographical context of Canadian attention. It has attempted to move beyond the old "Atlantic triangle," "Commonwealth," and "UN" cornerstones of Canadian external policy through its emphasis on more contacts with China and the Soviet Union, its emphasis on Francophone Africa and Latin America in its aid programs, and in its emphasis on increasing trade in the Pacific.

The trade relations with the Pacific have been discussed in a previous chapter. Yet what is so newly "internationalist" about Canada's aid program? The answer in part is found in the following statement by the head of the Canadian International Development Agency (February 4, 1971, before the House of Commons Standing Committee on External Affairs and Defence):

> Our programs in Asia, the Commonwealth of Africa and the Commonwealth Caribbean are becoming mature and well-rounded programs; . . . but it is in the two newest areas of work that . . . can most immediately shape the development of our assistance plans. This is one substantive reason why I intend to put stress upon the programs in Francophone Africa and Latin America. Let us speak about each of these programs in turn.

CIDA's program in Francophone Africa has until now been strongly oriented towards providing technical assistance. But a start has been made in implementing plans to support more innovative development projects. We need to put more impetus behind the delivery of capital assistance to the Francophone African states. From our figures of commitments of grants and loans, it is clear the impetus is beginning to build up; but again there is more to do. Our growing association with these countries is valuable in several ways. Through this association, we link ourselves as friends and partners with an important sector of the human family in Africa; through it we can use the great range of knowledge, experience and expertise that lie within the French-speaking communities across Canada for the benefit of the developing countries; and through it the Francophone Africa states can go beyond their past dependence for assistance on France and Belgium and find access to new relations around the world.

. . . There is a difference with CIDA's bilateral program in Latin America. It will be oriented, at least at the start, towards the supply of technical assistance. This is, however, balanced by the fact that the $60 million we have already advanced through the Inter-American Development Bank is being taken out in the form of capital assistance. Our new program of technical assistance will, as far as possible, be linked to work in education, agriculture, forestry and community development that may help to spread the benefits of change over a comparatively wide section of the people. The countries to which the CIDA teams of specialists have begun to go to identify specific projects – Colombia, Peru, Brazil and the Central American republics – are ones where the need for development assistance is great, and yet there is a planning organization within the countries to make good use of such assistance. This does not mean that we shall not offer similar assistance to other countries in Latin America in due course; we are also concerned to help in regional projects and in schemes of third-country training scholarships. There is nothing, therefore, exclusive about the list of countries the CIDA teams have started to visit.

The first three projects under the Canadian Government's new bilaterial assistance program for Latin America were finally announced in March, 1971. The $7 million to be provided through CIDA is aimed at improving food value of cassaua (a starch root crop), developing triticale (a cross between wheat and rye), and expanding the tele-communications sector in Guatemala. Also Canada's overall aid performance continues to improve in aggregate terms. Estimates for foreign aid disbursements for 1970-71 were $341.9 million for $362.9 million allocated. This is a marked improvement over previous years when there was a gap of $100 million between disbursements and allocations in 1968-69, and 1969-70 when disbursements reached $308 million, $30 million less than allocated. In 1970-71 Canada projected $176.8 million disbursements for Columbo Plan countries ($97 million in development loans, $13.1 million in grants and $67 million in food aid). Francophone Africa was projected at $35.9 million, Commonwealth Africa $36.6 million, and Commonwealth Caribbean $23.2 million.[9]

It is not "internationalism" that has diminished as a feature of Canadian external policy, it is the old "voluntarist" component of Canada's internationalism that appears to have diminished. The old Canadian voluntarist emphasis on acts of faith and "moral exhortion" has diminished. We have seen that Canada's defence priorities have shifted to an emphasis on "independence" and "sovereignty protection." The residual value of its NATO commitment seems primarily symbolic (that is, Canada continues to support Western Europe in a clear case of a Soviet attack) and for selfish motives (membership allows Canada to keep itself informed). The Trudeau Government has not ruled out peace-keeping roles for Canada but Lester Pearson's voluntarist readiness to contribute to peace-keeping is also clearly de-emphasized in both the Defence and Foreign Policy White Papers of the Trudeau Government. Canada's disillusionment with the results of "good intentions" in its peace-keeping in Cyprus, the Middle East and Southeast Asia (through the International Control Commission) has contributed to profound uneasiness in Canada with these ventures.

Canada's membership in the Commonwealth remains intact. But it is the voluntarist emphasis on moral action in this organization, so evident in both Lester Pearson's and John Diefenbaker's actions over Rhodesia and South Africa respectively, that has disappeared. Perhaps the clearest example of this new attitude is Prime Minister Trudeau's view of the Commonwealth which he articulated in a press conference before leaving for the Singapore Commonwealth Conference on January 5, 1971. He emphasized two themes: first, that he

[9] *Globe and Mail*, Jan. 12, 1971, p. 3.

could not and would not attempt to "pull off any miracles" by helping to reach a compromise on the issue of British arms sales to South Africa; and, second, he spoke at length about using the Conference to discuss "techniques of improving, shall we say, the Parliamentary democratic system. This to me is very fundamental: it is as important as any other issue."[10]

Compared with the past image of "active mediator" cultivated by Canadian Prime Ministers Pearson and Diefenbaker, the shift in emphasis is dramatic. While at the conference the Prime Minister argued further against "the helpful fixer" role for Canada and the Commonwealth by suggesting that the Commonwealth in the future ought to concentrate less on "immediate problems" and spend "two or three days in a general discussion of the world political situation and world economic situation." (Somewhat ironically, however, Mr. Trudeau ended up – against his will it appears – accepting a role on a committee to study the volatile issue of arms to South Africa.)

There are critics who see in the Trudeau Government's Water Pollution Prevention Act in 1970, which unilaterally declared Canada's right to police the Arctic archipelago up to zones of 100 miles, as another example of clear disinterest in "internationalism," an act of self-interest at total variance with the international community to say nothing of international law. Yet this too is a hopeless over-simplification. The House Standing Committee on External Affairs (with its Liberal majority), called for a unilateral declaration of sovereignty over the Arctic archipelago early in 1970. The Government responded by claiming a 100-mile zone for pollution prevention purposes. Claims by nation states for one purpose or another beyond the 3-mile limit are not new. Fifty-seven nations now claim limits of at least 12 miles. For example, in a note to Washington on April 16, 1970, Ottawa listed unilateral American claims beyond the 3-mile limit beginning in 1790 (when the Americans claimed customs jurisdiction to 12 miles) to an American action in 1932 when limits of up to 62 miles were claimed.

In any event, the Canadian Acts were not intended as declarations of sovereignty, nor were they intended to limit or rule out further Canadian claims. Ecological balance and pollution prevention in the Arctic are vital and inescapable challenges, and the Canadian action might have been forthcoming without the catalyst of the *Manhattan* voyage. Douglas Johnston, professor of law at the University of Toronto, outlines these issues:

Plant and animal life in the Arctic exists on a tenuous basis.

[10] Press Release, Prime Minister's Office, Jan. 5, 1971.

Serious damage to one species automatically threatens the existence of others. The chemical deficiencies of the region which lead to exceptionally slow processes of growth retard rehabilitation after serious environmental damage. At present the problems of protecting the Arctic land environments fall indisputably under national control and authority, though it may not be long before the logic of Arctic ecology brings at least some of the Arctic governments together to co-ordinate their environmental policies. This can be easily accomplished without provoking fears about the loss of national sovereignty and without seeming to challenge ancient principles of international law.

The problem of protecting the environment is, however, much more complicated in *marine* areas of the Arctic. . . . In short, . . . the extent of national environmental authority over Arctic waters has generally been regarded as limited by the traditional legal principle of the freedom of the high seas. . . . These issues were brought to a head by the Canadian government's initiative in introducing the Arctic Waters Pollution Prevention Act in April 1970. . . . The Act prohibits the deposit of waste of any kind in Arctic waters under Canadian jurisdiction and authorizes the Governor-in-Council to make appropriate regulations which would apply to all regardless of nationality. Violation constitutes a criminal offence and very strict penalties are prescribed. . . .

. . . Most significant of all, from the viewpoint of other countries, is the provision that Canadian jurisdiction for the limited purposes of this Act extends seaward 100 nautical miles from the nearest Canadian land, or as far as the line of equidistance between Canada and Greenland in areas where that is less than 100 miles out. It is essential to understand that this assertion of Canadian jurisdiction is not a claim to sovereignty. On the contrary, it is expressly limited to the specific purpose of pollution prevention. Nowhere, moreover, does the Act refer to territorial limits, but at the same time the Canadian government has enacted an amendment to the Territorial Sea and Fishing Zones Act, whereby Canada officially stakes its claim to a twelve-mile territorial sea in place of the former three-mile claim. Accordingly, the Arctic Waters Pollution Prevention Act can only be interpreted as a claim to limited national authority over an extensive area of the Arctic Ocean far beyond Canada's official territorial limits. To the extent that it purports to curtail the freedom of navigation on the high seas in that area, it seeks to exclude only those ships, Canadian or foreign, that refuse or fail to comply with Canadian pollution prevention regulations.[11]

Another example, not of a declining internationalism, but of little increase in voluntarism, is the mode of expenditure in Canada's aid programs. As noted, Canada's aid program shows an undoubted tendency to open windows on areas of the world hitherto rather hidden from Canadian foreign policy. This is an increase in internationalism. Yet the Canadian government's slowness in untying its aid hardly indicates a dramatic revival for the voluntarist impulse. The mixed character of Canada's performance is obvious in this further testimony of the CIDA head before the Commons Committee on External Affairs, February 4, 1971:

> A third concern I have, when studying the local impact of our assistance, is that the apparent Canadian interest has often been our preoccupation, to the clear disadvantage of the low-income country. The tying of much of our aid to procurement in Canada is without doubt a burden and a restriction upon these countries. We have been unable, except in special circumstances, to undertake projects that had a high local cost component; and this has been a serious obstacle to development in some cases. Several ministers of agriculture in African countries will testify to that. Some hard questions need to be asked for our own self-interest. In any case, are Canadian interests and local interests often – or indeed ever – irreconcilable? If development is seen in a long enough perspective, they surely are not. I am very happy that the foreign policy review last year gave CIDA a good deal of new flexibility which will enable us to pay more account to local interests by financing for example a higher proportion of local costs. As well, Canada is this year actively involved in the OECD Development Assistance Committee's study of ways to untie aid. . . .

Under the guidelines of the foreign policy review, we now tie about 50 per cent of our bilateral assistance to procurement in Canada. Meanwhile, we have recently been receiving back in the value of the contracts made by CIDA borrowers the equivalent of about 50 per cent of the funds we contribute on untied terms to that pool. CIDA and Industry, Trade and Commerce are making

[11] Douglas M. Johnston, "Canada's Artic Marine Environment: Problems of Legal Protection," *Behind the Headlines*, July, 1970, (Canadian Institute of International Affairs, Toronto), pp. 1, 2, 5.

a special effort to improve Canadian suppliers to win a fair share of the contracts awarded by multilateral institutions. Bread thrown on the waters does return to you, and not necessarily after many days. This is surely evidence that, even in considering the short term, Canadian interests and local interests are not irreconcilable.

Given the nature of Canada's international economic problems, this decline of voluntarism was perhaps inevitable. Also the unwillingness of increasing numbers of Canadians to perceive symbolic and voluntarist actions in foreign policy outside of North America as sufficient counterweights to the perceptions of U.S. influence in Canada may also have contributed to the decline in fashionability of voluntarist action outside of North America.

If the Trudeau approach to foreign policy cannot be called isolationist, simply less voluntarist than much of post-war Canadian foreign policy, there are those who argue that "internationalism" is impossible without "voluntarism." Yet a totally voluntarist foreign policy would be so ignorant of empirical restraints as to relegate Canada to the endless role of a Sisyphus or a Don Quixote. Surely the Canadian task in international affairs is one which balances the appropriate degree of voluntarism with self-interest. Carleton University Professor Peyton Lyon perhaps expresses best the tone and attitude such a balance would produce:

Certainly Canada would be foolish to boast about its crisis-solving capacity, to thrust its way uninvited into the disputes of others, to commit a large proportion of its resources to be ready for calls that may never come, to accept assignments on impossible terms, to break off valuable relationships in an attempt, probably vain, to enhance Canada's eligibility as an intermediary, or to make mediation and peacekeeping the sum total of foreign policy. But, so long as we steer clear of such obvious follies, why shun the blessed function of peacemaker? Why not recognize that Canada is a nation with some diplomatic, technical, and military strength, and a reasonable reputation for objectivity and inoffensiveness? And that, because of these characteristics, it may from time to time be invited to participate in international action to prevent or contain violence? Why not let the United Nations secretariat and other governments know, without fanfare, that Canada will continue to entertain such requests sympathetically?[12]

[12] Peyton Lyon, "The Trudeau Doctrine," *International Affairs*, Winter, 1970-71, p. 26.

The Findings
Panel Meeting of the Canada Study Project, Quebec City, June 12 and 13, 1971

The following is a summary of major issues as they were articulated in two panel meetings. The first was held in Toronto, the weekend of November 14 and 15, 1970. The second was held in Quebec City, the weekend of June 12 and 13, 1971.

The participants, drawn from commercial, governmental, and academic activities, became an integral part of this study from the beginning. Their deliberations were conducted on the basis of the issues raised in the preceding research materials.

Because the panelists were purposely chosen for their heterogeneous professional, regional, and, in some instances, national interests, it was expected that they would disagree substantially on many of the issues. That they did, and that their divergent views are represented herein is an accomplishment of one of the goals set down for this study. It is hoped that this defining of differences will contribute to better understanding of Canada's problems and at the same time suggest a variety of possible solutions.

CANADIANS WHO PARTICIPATED ON THE PANEL NOVEMBER 14, 1971 AT THE GUILD INN, SCARBOROUGH, ONTARIO AND THE CHATEAU FRONTENAC, QUEBEC CITY, JUNE 12, 13, 1971
JOHN DEUTSCH, PRINCIPAL, QUEEN'S UNIVERSITY (CHAIRMAN)

* **M. Jacques Barbeau**
Business lawyer from Quebec now in Vancouver after serving with the Department of Finance, Ottawa, and the Canadian Tax Foundation.

M. Hubert Guindon
Professor of Sociology, Sir George Williams University, Montreal

* **Mr. John W. Hetherington**
Recreation Products Division, Bombardier Limited, a fast growing, well-known Canadian-owned company

* **Miss Pauline Jewett**
One-time Liberal MP and presently with the Department of Political Science, Carleton University

* **Dr. Lloyd Barber**
Vice-President, University of Saskatchewan, and appointed member of the Council of the North-West Territories

* **Mr. John Harney**
Former Provincial Secretary, Ontario New Democratic Party, candidate for the leadership of the federal NDP in 1971

* **Dr. Trevor Lloyd**
Professor, Department of Geography, McGill University, member of the Arctic Institute of Canada

* **Mr. William Mahoney**
Vice-President, Canadian Labour Congress, President United Steel Workers of Canada

Mr. Peter C. Newman
Editor, *Maclean's* Magazine, noted Canadian writer, and member of the Committee for an Independent Canada

* **Mr. W. Runciman**
United Grain Growers of Canada, Winnipeg, Manitoba

* **Mr. J. G. McClelland**
President, McClelland and Stewart Limited, a leading Canadian-owned publishing company

* **Professor Denis Smith**
Department of Political Studies, Trent University, editor of *Journal of Canadian Studies*

* Those who attended the June 12, 13, 1971, meeting and from whose deliberations the *Findings* were prepared.

* **Mr. John Holmes**
  Director General, Canadian Institute of International Affairs, and formerly Under Secretary of State for External Affairs

* **M. Albert Legault**
  Professor of Political Science, Laval University, and author of several studies on Canadian defence policies

Dr. Guy Maclean
Dean of Arts, Dalhousie University, Halifax, Nova Scotia

* **Dr. A. W. R. Carrothers**
  President, University of Calgary, Calgary, Alberta

Mr. J. Allyn Taylor
President, Huron and Erie Canada Trust Company, London, Ontario

* **Professor Dale Thomson**
  Center of Canadian Studies, The Johns Hopkins University, Washington, D.C.

NON-CANADIANS WHO SERVED ON THE PANEL

* **Charles Albarez**
  Officer of Integration Advisor, Inter-American Development Bank

* **Mr. Isaac Auerbach**
  President, Auerbach Corporation Philadelphia, (a leading clearing house for the computer industry in the United States)

* **Hon. Willis C. Armstrong**
  Former U.S. Diplomat, in 1971 with U.S. Council of Chambers of Commerce, New York City

* **Mr. Nigel Lawson**
  Past editor of *The Spectator*, a noted British weekly

* **Mr. Robert Novak**
  Washington Syndicated Columnist

* **Mr. John Dickey**
  President Emeritus, Dartmouth College, New Hampshire

* **Mr. Mario A. Cámpora**
  Department of Foreign Affairs, Argentina

Dr. Jiro Tokuyama
Nomura Research Institute for Technology and Economics, Tokyo

* **Mr. Shigeru Otsuka**
  Executive Director, Japan Trade Center, New York City

THE FINDINGS OF THE PANEL

National Economic Development and Public Policy

1. The assumption that almost all foreign investment in Canada is consistent with legitimate Canadian needs distinguished the postwar mood of Canada up to the mid-sixties. With the arrival of the seventies this assumption will be continually challenged and increasing scepticism about unrestrained foreign investment will be a feature of the years to come. Pressure for government leadership to stop the erosion of Canada's economic independence will vary from little or no pressure in some provinces to considerable pressure in others.

The panel explained this asymmetrical attitude of regions by the fact that Canada is made up of diverse interconnected regions: some are completely undeveloped, (such as parts of the north); some are developed unidimensionally (for example, in resource extraction), and are insistent on more diversification of their economic activity; and some regions are so well-developed and diversified, such as Toronto and Montreal, as to be best characterized as primarily post-industrial in nature. Each region has different priorities for economic development and this makes many broad government policies popular with some regions, unpopular with others.

2. While recognizing these differing priorities, the panel argued that policy which conceives of the whole country as undeveloped is no longer appropriate. The positive incentives for foreign investment that existed in the 1950's and 1960's are no longer desirable. It must be recognized that there is now a considerable pool of educated personnel, labour, expertise, and capital in Canada, which makes heavy importation of these factors of production from the outside less necessary than previously. If, however, these Canadian factors of production are to be more equitably distributed among regions, it will be necessary to recognize that foreign investment must increasingly assume a minority position and be directed more to regional needs. Canadians must also be encouraged to exercise more participation and control in their economy even if this means disincentives on the investment of Canadian savings abroad and on lending by Canadian banks to finance foreign take-overs.

3. There was also a strong insistence by some on the panel that in order to prevent inadequate returns from resource industries, Canada

must study its options very carefully; for example, whether increased taxes on, or increased Canadian ownership of, natural resource industries is desirable. The panel agreed that more processing of natural resources must take place in Canada and urged as well a federal government strategy discouraging the miniature replica effect of secondary industry with its inefficiencies, lack of economy of scale, and low export incentives.

4. Some panelists argued further that once the facts of foreign (especially U.S.) ownership and control were better known across Canada there would be a public consensus – including even most provincial governments – for more vigorous activity to reverse the trend of foreign ownership and control. They pointed, for example, to the steady change of the Canadian Labour Movement from an organic relationship with their American counterparts to a fraternal one, and also to the concern of young Canadians in all parts of Canada about Canadian independence.

5. The panel emphasized the increasingly "nationalistic" context in which decisions on economic development and independence will be made in future, in contrast with past Canadian policy. Canadian panelists stressed that the impending major decisions on these issues will be decided less on purely technical or managerial assessments, and more on political value judgements based on the assumption that if an objective is important enough politically, governments in one way or another, will find the capital to pursue the objective. Some panelists argued that a policy is needed on the investment of Canadians' private savings in order to ensure that some of these savings will be used for purposes more conducive to public needs, especially for the relief of unemployment, regional economic development, and for increased Canadian ownership of the economy.

6. Several panelists urged strongly that Canadians should be encouraged to analyse more closely the key institutions for independence and creativity of mind and purpose, namely the universities. To many on the panel, Canadian universities appeared to be too much dominated by the American models and subject-delineation, and that development of any viable long-term sense of unique development will depend on both a more cosmopolitan, and a more clearly defined, Canadian notion of what a university should do for society, its graduates, and its faculty.

7. It was generally agreed by the panel that Canadians, even the most ardent nationalists, are not advocating national autarky (complete self-sufficiency). They recognize that for economic progress, and for some assurance of success from rationalization of industry, particularly of specialized manufacturing, that considerable integration with markets of other countries is inevitable. Also it would be a gross misreading of the forces of economic nationalism in Canada to describe them as "militant" in a narrow ethnic or cultural sense. The forces of economic nationalism spring more from an impulse for greater self-reliance than from a militant arousal of narrow nationalist passion.

8. Besides the structure of Canada's manufacturing sector, and the lack of export incentives that may exist for certain types of foreign-owned subsidiaries, several other vital trade tactics seemed, to some panelists, to be neglected by Canada. Suggestions for reform varied widely: Canada should develop trading companies, similar to Japan's Mitsubishi to facilitate buying, selling, financing, and exchanging in unaccustomed markets; that greater trade contacts with developing countries and communist nations would help Canada to break out of some of the old restraints on its trade; that Canada, like Japan, should establish a combines policy which encourages fewer producers, longer production runs, and vigorous export performance; and finally, that Canada should use its bilingual capacity and high educational performance to monitor, study, and adopt the basic innovations of other nations, and encourage its technically-skilled people, not simply its trade officers, to travel regularly abroad in search of new ideas and developments in their fields.

9. Finally, several non-Canadian panelists pointed out that, in their view, one of the most potent government policies in the long and short run for Canadian independence, related to the broad questions of fiscal and monetary policy and the action of the Canadian government to float its dollar.

Canadian Foreign Policy

1. Canadian foreign policy in the seventies will undoubtedly emphasize economic dimensions rather than the security and political dimensions of the past. Canadians are beginning to understand that Canada is a major economic trading power, and that this will necessitate increased understanding, in educational institutions, the press, and in

government, of these dimensions of international activity. It also implies a greater Canadian willingness to contribute to real solutions concerning the differences in the Commonwealth, the UN, and elsewhere in negotiations on trade agreements with developing nations. It also implies that Canada's contacts with the Soviet Union and China should be increased to enhance Canada's trade options. The panel did not consider it useful to consider the Pacific as an "area" in itself, but insisted that it be considered as a vital new dimension for Canadian external activity, at the same time recognizing that each Pacific nation affords very different challenges to Canadian external policy, especially in trade.

2. Americans should not assume that Canadian interests are everywhere identical to those of the United States. Canada's pursuit of its national interests, and its efforts to change its laws and incentives to meet the needs of its mature economy will be prompted, not by anti-Americanism, but by the unprecedented necessity in Canada to solve its new internal problems. Canada's approach to these problems will have repercussions in the United States, but Americans would greatly err if they perceived these repercussions to be the motive of Canadian policy, especially on the question of economic ownership.

3. It is no doubt likely that Canada will continue to receive puzzled attention in the U.S. and elsewhere if it does not define the parts of its economy and social life it deems essential to "basic national services" in both its developed and undeveloped economy, and continues to oscillate between affirmations of interdependence and independence without establishing political values and criteria for delineating which is appropriate.

4. The challenge of the Arctic to Canada is, the panel felt, more than a challenge of underdevelopment. They agreed that there was no realistic challenge to Canada's legal sovereignty in the north, and that the 12-mile limit is an accepted international reality. The real problem lies in control of the northwest passages by Canada. But as this is a technical, and not a policy matter, Canada should be willing to collaborate in a new world organization for pollution and other controls in the far north if this helps to solve the technical problems of control.

5. There also seemed to be general agreement that the defence priorities of the federal government will be: a) surveillance of Canadian territory, especially the coasts; b) bilateral co-operation with the U.S. in

continental defence; c) continued participation in NATO and peace-keeping actions; and d) internal security. There was considerable disagreement among the panelists over b and c. Some panelists argued that the assumption of the inevitability of an east-west military struggle was unrealistic, and therefore, Canada should not participate in NATO and NORAD; others argued that such a danger was real, and therefore, Canada should participate.

Quebec

1. The panel did not attempt to predict the ultimate future of Quebec in the Canadian federal system. It did note, however, that there are powerful arguments for a more decentralized and more flexible federalism. The panel also deplored the not infrequent tendency of Ontario to assume that its priorities reflect the priorities of Canada as a whole, and the tendency of the English-speaking press and sometimes the federal government to interpret Quebec's proposals for jurisdictional, tax, or fiscal reform as "balkanist" when similar, if not equally decentralized, proposals from other provinces are not similarly interpreted. This bifurcation makes it difficult for Quebec to be perceived as constructive in the constitutional or federalist debate and therefore further contributes to misunderstanding between Quebec and the rest of Canada.

2. The panel was clearly split, not so much on the intrinsic desirability, but on the feasibility and costs of attempts to integrate the two major cultures across Canada in most levels of education, and in the federal public service outside of Ottawa. It was felt by most panelists, but not all, that it is probably impossible to install the presence of the French culture and to integrate the two cultures in those areas of Canada where the French language is not spoken, and where the use of French would amount to an act of artificial insemination. It seemed clear also that the major political parties in Quebec do not find this question decisive in the relations of Quebec with the rest of Canada.

3. The panel also recognized the extent to which some of Quebec's more vital concerns now bear rather directly on questions of Canadian external policy. Quebec's need for capital will constantly drive it to search outside Canada if it is not supplied from within. Any trade or development policy from Ottawa designed to encourage more manufacturing and processing in Canada must emphasize, far more than

ever before, a more equitable share of such activity for Quebec. Another development, noted by French Canadians on the panel, was that as Ottawa increased its contracts with Francophone nations, and as Ottawa and Quebec increased the number of French Canadians serving abroad, Quebec began to discover more contracts and markets for its cultural, educational, and economic skills. It seems clear, therefore, that the attentive public in Quebec, even though greatly troubled by domestic problems, are becoming increasingly interested in external policy.

Panelists' Comments

Willis C. Armstrong, United States Council of Chambers of Commerce, New York City

Being one of the American members of the panel was an interesting experience. The background material is informative and deserves wide circulation among Canadians and Americans. The chapter on Quebec political trends is especially noteworthy. The draft *Findings* presented to the panel was a paper of less intellectual appeal, and the draft presented after the panel discussions of June, 1971, is equally uninteresting, although it reflects with reasonable accuracy the sentiments expressed by the most articulate Canadians on the panel.

An American expresses himself with hesitation on the matters dealt with in the *Findings*. Questions of national sovereignty are highly emotional for the nationals concerned and often difficult for the foreigner to comprehend. Questions of relations between French and other Canadians are something of a family matter where the outsider's only helpful attitude is one of sympathetic silence.

With these caveats clearly expressed, and recognizing that it is for Canadians to decide what their policies and actions should be, I nevertheless venture a few comments, intended to be friendly, unselfish, and constructive, although they may not so appear in the eye of a Canadian beholder. In so doing, I refrain from taking a position on the *Findings* as a whole.

First, a general observation on the panel itself. The Canadian business "establishment" – national and international – seemed almost totally unrepresented in the June panel meeting. The academic community was well represented, and there was a strong contingent of articulate nationalists of Canadian (not French) extraction. Quebec and French Canada seemed under-represented quantitatively, although qualitatively they did not suffer from their panelists and visitors. The basic tenor of the discussions was essentially that of a seminar conducted mostly by academics from Ontario. These are points which the reader should bear in mind. The foreigners on the panel were diversified in their views, and varied in their knowledge of Canada. Their views are but little reflected in the *Findings*, perhaps for understandable reasons.

Section 1 (National Development and Public Policy), states quite accurately the views of those Canadians on the panel who were most articulate in advocating a position of economic nationalism. Although there are references in paragraphs (7) and (8) to the importance of Canada's world trading position as an element in the performance of the Canadian economy, it does not deal, fundamentally, with the economics of Canada. Rather it concentrates on the possibility of management of the Canadian economy to serve certain non-economic and primarily political objectives. It advocates control over outward and inward movements of investment capital, a diminution in the amount of equities available to investors from abroad, severe treatment of existing foreign interests, and an ideological approach to national economic questions. This approach is justified in the text by the assertion that this is what many Canadians want, especially the young; it is further implied that such management of the Canadian economy and society will give considerable psychological satisfaction to Canadians, although it is conceded that areas in need of further investment (read the Maritimes, Newfoundland, the Prairies, British Columbia, the Arctic, Quebec, and Northern Ontario) might not derive the same psychological satisfaction as other Canadians who are leaders in this movement.

What is the purpose of economic activity? Normally one thinks of jobs, goods, and services for the population. Judged by this standard, previous and present Canadian policies have succeeded as well as, or better than, those of most countries. Aggressive policies have been pursued in the essential field of foreign trade. Canada's material resources, human skills, services infrastructure, and monetary reserves make it an unusually rich country, not to mention the level of personal income. There is hardly a country anywhere so fortunate, so independent, and so envied.

If one is to redirect economic policy toward certain non-economic ends, one should be obliged to demonstrate that the gains will be worth the cost. The benefits may well be political, and the costs economic. It is for the Canadians to decide what the calculations show, to assess the cost, and to act accordingly. Asserting, as do the *Findings*, that basic changes in economic policy are essential for political reasons assumes either that there will be no cost in economic terms or that any cost will be so minimal as to raise no question concerning its wisdom. Implicit in the reasoning set forth in Section 1 is the bland assumption that Canada can have its cake and eat it too.

This may be more possible for Canada than for some less fortunate countries, but one must remember economic principle number one, to the effect that there is no such thing as a free lunch.

Essentially the fault of the *Findings* is that they represent the views of articulate political scientists who do not want to be bothered by such unpleasant economic questions as the following, which Canadian businessmen, farmers, workers, bankers, and economists might well pose:

1. If Canada discriminates against foreign capital now invested in Canada, by changing the rules under which it was originally invited, what will be the impact on Canada's growth rate, standard of living, and international economic position?

2. If Canada lays down rules affecting the future inflow of capital, or the outflow of Canadian investment abroad, what will happen to the level of business activity, economic growth in areas which want it, unemployment, and the balance of payments?

3. If Canada secedes from the North American common market for capital, what kind of Canadian capital market will remain, and how well can it serve Canadian requirements?

4. Could Canada maintain and expand its access to foreign markets while restricting the access of foreigners to Canadian markets?

These issues could be stated in any number of ways, but the essential point is that if a profound change in economic policy is contemplated, those Canadians primarily responsible for producing Canada's goods and services, and paying Canada's taxes, are entitled to the most rigorous economic analysis of the possible consequences as a basis for their decision. At no point do the *Findings* refer to the need for such a study, and at no point do those whose views are reported in the *Findings* appear to indicate any need to consult more widely among their compatriots.

Section 2 of the *Findings*, on Foreign Policy, raises fewer questions than Section 1. In its initial paragraph it emphasizes the importance of economic matters, but does not recognize this point as in any way contradictory to the proposals of Section 1, which in fact it may well be. Its appeal to Americans not to regard Canadian nationalist manifestations as anti-American will be salted down for future reference by American readers, who will draw their own conclusions. Canadians might well recognize that Americans who are informed about Canada are quite used to hearing this suggestion, and will not find in it anything new. To them there are some interesting myths in Canadian folklore, which include the idea that because there is a great deal of foreign ownership there is therefore great foreign political influence, the thought that Canadians are innocent and defenceless in a world of superpowers, the impression that the United States wishes to annex Canada, and the theme that the Canadian government does not effectively advance Canadian interests. These are examples of some things that Canadians, some Canadians, sincerely believe as an essential element of a nationalist faith. To a rational American these things are manifestly untrue; but if they help keep Canada together and give it a sense of purpose and self-confidence, Americans can see the point in avoiding argument. All nationalist movements are built in part on myth; what we really need are some better myths that will support the cause of international amity and understanding.

Section 3 deals with Quebec and reflects the discussion very well. An outsider present at the discussion may be pardoned for reflecting that it was essentially an Anglo-Canadian discussion which sought sympathetically to examine the question, while regarding French Canada as a somewhat alien element rather hard to understand and handle. One would hope that there would be, some day, a Canadian discussion in which French Canada appeared as an integral part of the country; but communication must improve before this sort of discussion emerges. To an outsider there are many Canadas, all attractive and interesting; there is also one Canada, easier to perceive from the outside than it is for those within. May their perception improve.

*J. Allyn Taylor, Chairman and President,
Canada Trust-Huron and Erie*

I am not entirely in accord with the first section of the *Findings*, which deals with National Economic Development and Public Policy.

True, it doesn't reflect the emotional brand of negative nationalism that is evident in some sectors of Canadian thinking today. And I entirely agree that foreign investors must understand the need to be sensitive to Canada's national aspirations. But such suggestions as

"the positive incentives for foreign investment . . . that existed previously . . . are no longer desirable," and "there is now a considerable
pool of . . . capital in Canada . . . so as to make heavy importation . . .
from the outside less necessary than previously," imply an unrealistic
degree of capital self-sufficiency.

The fact is we do not have sufficient capital to meet our needs,
either now or in the foreseeable future. We must choose between wise
utilization of foreign capital or much slower economic growth. If that
growth does not at least keep pace with population increases then
rising unemployment and a declining standard of social services will
result and we will be in trouble.

The important thing, as the *Findings* suggest, is to encourage the
use of our own savings in the ownership of enterprises involved in
Canada's growth. This calls for a political and economic environment
that will make such ownership desirable and beneficial.

Nevertheless, I do not believe the *Findings* give sufficient emphasis
to the huge chunks of foreign investment capital that will also be
needed for the development of the country.

Under Canadian Foreign Policy I fear the phrase "our country is
a major economic trading power" is far from the fact, though I have
no quarrel with the conclusions that follow. We are dependent on
trade – relatively more perhaps than any other developed nation – but
we are not a major factor by world standards. As a nation we are a
small contender facing a polarization of trade among trading blocs
throughout the world. Our national fervour must be tempered accordingly.

*Shigeru Otsuka, Executive Director, Japan Trade Center,
New York City*

In view of the present economic situation where the Canadian economy is placed under American domination, the *Findings* are, as a matter
of general rule, very relevant and appropriate.

I am firmly convinced that as long as the international borderlines
solemnly exist among the nations, economic infiltration by one nation
into the other should be so adjusted that the economic sovereignty of
the latter be maintained. It is therefore extremely worthwhile noting
that "Canadians must be encouraged to exercise more participation
and control in the Canadian economy."

It is also significant to note, however, that the existing alien interests have already been closely incorporated into the Canadian economy to the extent that abrupt or unplanned alienation of the foreign interests from the Canadian economic integrity "to be participated in and controlled by Canadians" would impair the whole Canadian economy. Accordingly Canadian economic independence should be pursued only in the manner that her total economic efficiency could best be sustained to the advantage of the Canadian national interest.

The pursuit of Canadian economic nationalism should be undertaken lest her economic competitiveness should be lost on the international market or economic isolationism should ensue as a result of the loss of international viability.

It seems to be a very constructive notion that Canada should aim at developing trading companies similar to Japan's Mitsubishi. It is to be noted, however, that far-reaching overseas networks of the trading companies are a prerequisite to their expansion and prosperity, thus necessitating large initial investments to put the notion in practice with the maximum efficiency.

I would like to add that the success of the Japanese trading companies lies also in their versatile business lines including producing activities. They are engaged in strenuous attempts to either diversify their business activities in order to catch up with the swelling world trade and economy, or in attempts to become less vulnerable to fluctuating business cycles.

John S. Dickey, President Emeritus, Dartmouth College,
New Hampshire

Since the *Findings* of the panel are properly focused on Canadian national objectives and policies, and since I was privileged to participate in one of its sessions, primarily as an American student of the Canadian-U.S. relationship, I shall refrain from joining in what is essentially a prescription for Canada.

I might, however, use the vantage point of an outsider to make several observations:

First, as we all should know, nationalism is heady stuff, hard to take in moderation, albeit necessary as an ingredient of national independence. At this stage in the development of a more mature international community, all concerned, including especially perhaps the U.S., have a stake in an independent Canada sustained by a healthy nationalism. The U.S. has a contribution of more sensitive understanding and restraint to make, but the primary input of wisdom and self-discipline must, of course, be Canadian.

Second, I suspect that few in Canada or elsewhere yet understand how cross-grained some forms of contemporary nationalism and, paradoxically, a more "decentralized federalism" may prove to be in respect to national objectives aimed at greater nationalization of Canadian productivity and a more rewarding Canadian participation in the international community.

Albert Legault, Department of Political Science, Laval University

Il n'est pas de conclusions au rapport général dont j'aimerais me dissocier. Je me permets donc de le compléter par quelques remarques sur la nature de notre politique étrangère et de nos obligations militaires.

Le livre blanc sur la défense canadienne d'août 1971 démontre abondamment qu'il existe moultes menaces de nature non-militaire qui risquent de porter atteinte à la souveraineté du Canada, notamment dans le domaine de la pollution, de l'exploitation indue de nos ressources aquatiques, ou encore de la mise en valeur de nos nappes sous-marines pétrolifères. Les grandes puissances, d'autre part, face à un équilibre nucléaire parfaitement réalisé, ont conclu à bon droit qu'il fallait juxtaposer au système de la "guerre nucléaire impensable" la formule de la paix nucléaire négociée. Les petites et moyennes puissances, pour leur part, n'étant nullement impliquées dans ce processus sinon que très indirectement, n'ont plus qu'à se rabattre sur ces tâches plus immédiatement nationales. Voilà un droit que personne ne leur contestera.

Quant à l'orientation générale de notre politique étrangère qui consiste à ménager tout à la fois la chèvre et le chou, à nous orienter "tous azimuths," à nous considérer comme une plaque tournante aux charnières de l'Europe, de l'Asie, et de l'Amérique, je n'ai rien essentiellement à y redire sauf que nous risquons de devenir, dans ces conditions, une seconde Suisse nord-américaine. Nous risquons surtout de nous "ennuyer" faute de trouver un défi à relever à la mesure des aspirations de notre pays. Il serait grand temps qu'à côté des notions fort générales de prospérité, de croissance économique et de "qualité" de la vie humaine, l'on pense une fois pour toutes à définir les dimensions de notre nationalisme, autrement que par simple opposition aux Etats-Unis.

Bien sûr, nous ne sommes plus le premier grenier à blé du monde, mais les richesses qui jonchent notre sous-sol sont incommensurables. Bien sûr, nous entendons nous protéger contre les convoitises qu'elles suscitent, mais ressentons du même coup une frustration permanente à ne pouvoir les exploiter nous-mêmes. En fait, le Canada n'est autre chose qu'un Japon atlantique, à la différence que nous avons des ressources qu'il ne possède pas, et que nous n'avons pas la main-d'oeuvre et le potentiel démographique qu'il possède. Nous ne sommes donc, comme Herman Kahn l'a déjà souligné avec humour, qu'une "puissance régionale sans région." De là découle l'inaliénable ambiguité du Canada constamment à la recherche de son identité.

John Holmes, Director General, Canadian Institute of International Affairs

If, as is suggested in the *Findings,* Canadian foreign policy in the "seventies will emphasize the economic dimensions of external policy more than the security and political dimensions," this is because economic questions will loom larger in international relations. Canada is not an economic superpower, but it is certainly a major power and its voice is important in the Group of Ten, or in the World Bank, or GATT because the volume of its trade and investment, and the importance of its currency are of international consequence. It is to be hoped that in this emerging era Canadians will acquire sufficient confidence in their international status to act with assurance and with a due sense of responsibility for international structures and world development. To do so it will be necessary to shake off the neurotic obsession with independence which has paralysed the Canadian will in a period when a superstitious importance still clings to political and military power.

There are strong arguments for reducing foreign ownership of the Canadian economy, but it should be noted, nevertheless, that the Canadian voice internationally is strong and independent regardless of the nature of this ownership. On the law of the sea, Arctic sovereignty, the Kennedy Round, monetary issues, and in the World Bank the Canadian voice is not unduly inhibited by foreign ownership, and it is strengthened by the extraordinary wealth of the Canadian economy. Those who insist that Canadian international policy is subordinated to that of the United States, whether they do so because they rejoice in or abhor American investment, do a great disservice because their analysis can be self-fulfilling. The view that Canada is a satellite is much more strongly held in Canada than abroad.

We cannot have it both ways. We cannot rejoice in being an economic major power and retain the traditional notion of ourselves as a lesser and undeveloped country, licensed by its weakness to abuse the great powers and belligerently protect its own national interest. We may see ourselves as smaller and poorer beside the United States, but in the eyes of the world at large we are exceedingly rich, and in terms of relative population and resources, perhaps the most fortunate country in the world. An excessive preoccupation, therefore, with hoarding our resources, extending our coastal waters in a mood of aggrieved nationalism is not only unbecoming but unacceptable. As far as our future is concerned the question of controlling our own resources *vis-à-vis* the United States is important but subsidiary. The real issues are how twenty-one million people can sit on all this land and all these resources and get away with it.

Peter C. Newman, Editor of Maclean's *Magazine*

I agree with the basic thrust of the recommendations but it seems to me that there is one thing missing. The trouble is that the conquest of any nation takes place not on battle fields or even in business board rooms, but in the souls of the people and in the minds of their leaders. Colonization is not an isolated act. Conquest requires surrender. Without surrender colonization is ultimately impossible, as in Vietnam for instance. The choice between surrender and resistance is dictated not by material resources or available manpower, but by a state of psychological abdication. Surrender is essentially an admission that something is lacking and a willingness to take the chance that the conqueror will be able to supply it. This has been the Canadian experience. The Americans are in the process of taking over Canada, not because they are conquerors, but because Canadians are so ready to surrender. It's that terrible ingrained uncertainty in us, the

---

absence of knowing who we are and why we are here, which is gradually depriving us of nationhood.

So if we are to regain that nationhood, it will be up to us both as individuals and as a nation to find a reason for its existence. The Americans cannot define the Canadian soul for us.

Mario A. Cámpora, Department of Foreign Affairs, Argentina

The second part of this book which refers to external realities is not properly reflected in the *Findings*.

The external sector has acquired a fundamental importance in the life of the state as a consequence of new international conditions which have transformed the society of nations into a highly competitive and interdependent one. What is more, a self-sufficient state is a Utopian objective. For since the Industrial and Technological Revolutions have made possible industrial and economic processes of such magnitude, no individual state can, by itself, exist because of a lack of the scientific, material and economic resources required by such processes; *viz*, electronics, atomic and space technology, etc. Because of this, states need the external sector in order to reach the high degrees of development offered by contemporary industrial and technological advances. At the same time, a richer international life, a consequence of the growing involvement of the state beyond its national frontiers, has created the necessity of an international co-operation which tends to formulate norms to regulate the conduct of the states in the society of nations. The fact that this co-operation must include such areas as environmental conservation, is a significant index of the high degree of interdependence existent among nations.

Therefore, the external sector has reached an unprecedented importance, and *the defence of the national interest in a highly competitive and interdependent international society requires, above all, the preparation of the national society to act competently in the international sphere.*

The development described above is aptly illustrated by what is said in the section on external realities concerning Canada.

Nevertheless, in our opinion, the *Findings* do not bring out sufficiently, the importance of the external factor, in spite of the questions of economic interdependence, security and defence commitments, preservation of sovereignty in the Arctic regions, and the area of pollution control, all of which are mentioned in the second part, and which show the degree to which the external sector conditions a fuller realization of national interests.

A. M. Runciman, President of the United Grain Growers Limited, Winnipeg

The author of this book, and the panelists involved in the *Findings* are not timid. They have attempted to "grasp Canada as a whole" – a large, difficult, even impossible task. The fact that they do not wholly succeed is, therefore, not very surprising.

Their problem lies, for the most part, in their very concept of Canada. In Chapter 1, Canada is described as a "condominium," or "a multiple unit organization comprising individual components that afford a high degree of social, economic, and political diversity." What emerges from both the book and the *Findings*, however, is a very different kind of Canada. Far from being a condominium, the Canada which the author and most of the panelists describe is really nothing more than a market stall. And a very special kind of market stall it is: a tiny market stall which operates on a concession basis – one small counter on the fringe of a huge American supermarket. The author may have hoped for a condominium, but both the book and *Findings* indicate that all they got was a market stall.

Such a metaphor is clearly not an accurate description of Canada. But it might be one if we were concerned only about the relationship between the market stall and the supermarket. In other words, they *have* attempted to "grasp Canada as a whole," but both panelists (most of the Canadians being from eastern Canada), and author see it primarily in terms of its relationship to the United States. (One is tempted to ask if they would describe the USSR and China in the same way.) This approach would be fine if their audience were American – and possibly this is the audience. But for Canadians, and for Americans who wish to use Canadians discovering their identity as the basis for understanding Canada, it is only a partial image.

Canadians, and I believe those who really wish to know Canada as a Canadian would know it, require a very different approach. If Canada is to be grasped as a whole they require nothing less than a detailed examination of the relationship between the component parts of Canada – specifically between their part of the country and central Canada. The author has good intentions, but both he and the seminar participants failed to provide this analysis. Instead, we see trotted out the usual regional descriptions of the economic life of Canada which may be found in any standard textbook.

Indirectly, however, by concentrating so much on the problems of Canada's industrial heartland, Ontario and Quebec, the author and the panelists have raised the central problem facing those Canadians living on the fringe. How does one live with the central Canadian post-industrial Juggernaut?

Neither the book nor the *Findings* provide ANSWERS. But for western Canadians this is the question. The book and the *Findings* concentrate so intensely on the industrial, commercial, and investment problems of central Canada, that they unwittingly adopt the viewpoint of central Canada. They do so not only in relation to the rest of Canada but towards the United States as well. Consider the reaction of people in the U.S. mid-west if Canadians used impressions from New York State as indicative of their situation. Consider the statement that in many aspects the Canadians of the Prairies have more in common with the people of Minnesota, North Dakota and Montana than they have with the people of Ontario and Quebec. Here are some examples of how the central Canadian viewpoint is adopted: ·

1. Quebec. The book and *Findings* deal with great insight, imagination, and sympathy with Quebec's problems and her relationship to the rest of Canada. With Ontario, Quebec comprises the largest labour pool and consumer market in Canada. Her political problems are a threat to that economic unity. But Quebec is not a Western problem. At least Westerners are not inclined to see it that way. Parochial? Regional? Perhaps. But the West is a long way from Quebec and shares few economic, social, or cultural problems.

2. Foreign (American) Investment. The amount of American investment in Canada may be a problem for Ontario and Quebec which are, unlike the West, saturated with capital. Moreover, central Canadians are concerned about specific kinds of foreign investment which tend, as they see it, to infringe on Canadian sovereignty. Fine – for them. But western Canadians are concerned that their economies become more stable through diversification and industrialization. Economic nationalism, however understated and mild (as it is in the